411 SAT
ESSAY PROMPTS
AND WRITING QUESTIONS

411 SAT
ESSAY PROMPTS AND WRITING QUESTIONS

LearningExpress®

NEW YORK

Library of Congress Catologing-in-Publication Data:
411 essay prompts and writing questions.
  p. cm.
 Includes bibliographical references and index.
 ISBN 1-57685-562-7 (alk. paper)
 1. SAT (Educational test)—Study guides. 2. Universities and colleges—
United States—Entrance examinations—Study guides.
LB2353.57.A138 2006
378.1'662—dc22

                    2006012695

Printed in the United States of America

9 8 7 6 5 4 3 2 1

ISBN 1-57685-562-7

For information on LearningExpress, other LearningExpress products, or bulk sales, please write to us at:
 LearningExpress
 55 Broadway
 8th Floor
 New York, NY 10006

Or visit us at:
 www.learnatest.com

Contents ▶

411 SAT
ESSAY PROMPTS
AND WRITING QUESTIONS

Introduction ▶

As any scary book or movie proves repeatedly, the most frightening thing anyone usually has to face is the unknown or unexpected. If you know that you are going to be attacked by a hostile alien from Pluto, you can prepare for it with the appropriate high-tech weaponry. If you know that a crazed former high school sweetheart looking for revenge is waiting in the basement, you can call 911 and then run. It's the not knowing what is around the corner that is usually the most intimidating.

The same is true when it comes to taking the SAT. If you don't know what the SAT is going to be like or what questions it is going to ask, your imagination can really scare you into thinking it is much worse than it is or lead you to believe it is something it isn't. By taking the time to study and understand what actually is on the SAT (versus what you imagine might be), you will be prepared. You will know exactly what to expect and thus, how to prepare (and how not to).

411 SAT Essay Prompts and Writing Questions will show you what is going to be in the SAT Writing section, as well as what you need to know to ace it. It takes the mystery—and thus the fear—out of the whole study process and gives you the information you need to get a stronger, higher score.

Following that theme, let's start off by removing the unknown from how this book is designed. Here is what we are going to do:

- take a look at some of the basic strategies of taking the SAT, such as using the process of elimination and coping with test anxiety
- explain in-depth each of the four different kinds of writing challenges the SAT gives you and how to address each one, including the essay portion
- give you hundreds (yes, hundreds!) of examples of the multiple-choice questions and writing prompts you will find on the test and show you how to figure out the correct responses to them
- discuss how the SAT is scored

With these tools, you can walk into the classroom and when you see the Writing section of the SAT, it will be like seeing an old friend.

Ready? Don't worry. This is much easier than facing an alien or former sweetheart.

Pretest

To find out how well you already know what you will be tested on, take a brief pretest. The following 25 questions will include:

- 9 identifying sentence errors questions
- 12 improving sentences questions
- 3 improving paragraphs questions
- 1 writing prompt

Without doing any more reading or studying, take this test and see how you do. After you have read the following chapters and have had the chance to learn the rules, there will be a posttest. It will be exciting to see what improvements you have made!

Ready? Make sure you've already had a drink, gone to the bathroom, taken some deep breaths, and relaxed yourself. Even though you won't have to do this test on a time limit (like you will on the SAT), do it as fast as you can. On the official test, you will only have 35 minutes to do 60 questions. At that rate, this one should only take you about 15 minutes or less. Pick up that sharpened number two pencil and see how it goes. Good luck!

PRETEST

1.	ⓐ	ⓑ	ⓒ	ⓓ	ⓔ
2.	ⓐ	ⓑ	ⓒ	ⓓ	ⓔ
3.	ⓐ	ⓑ	ⓒ	ⓓ	ⓔ
4.	ⓐ	ⓑ	ⓒ	ⓓ	ⓔ
5.	ⓐ	ⓑ	ⓒ	ⓓ	ⓔ
6.	ⓐ	ⓑ	ⓒ	ⓓ	ⓔ
7.	ⓐ	ⓑ	ⓒ	ⓓ	ⓔ
8.	ⓐ	ⓑ	ⓒ	ⓓ	ⓔ
9.	ⓐ	ⓑ	ⓒ	ⓓ	ⓔ
10.	ⓐ	ⓑ	ⓒ	ⓓ	ⓔ

11.	ⓐ	ⓑ	ⓒ	ⓓ	ⓔ
12.	ⓐ	ⓑ	ⓒ	ⓓ	ⓔ
13.	ⓐ	ⓑ	ⓒ	ⓓ	ⓔ
14.	ⓐ	ⓑ	ⓒ	ⓓ	ⓔ
15.	ⓐ	ⓑ	ⓒ	ⓓ	ⓔ
16.	ⓐ	ⓑ	ⓒ	ⓓ	ⓔ
17.	ⓐ	ⓑ	ⓒ	ⓓ	ⓔ
18.	ⓐ	ⓑ	ⓒ	ⓓ	ⓔ
19.	ⓐ	ⓑ	ⓒ	ⓓ	ⓔ
20.	ⓐ	ⓑ	ⓒ	ⓓ	ⓔ

21.	ⓐ	ⓑ	ⓒ	ⓓ	ⓔ
22.	ⓐ	ⓑ	ⓒ	ⓓ	ⓔ
23.	ⓐ	ⓑ	ⓒ	ⓓ	ⓔ
24.	ⓐ	ⓑ	ⓒ	ⓓ	ⓔ

► Questions

The following sentences test your knowledge of grammar, usage, diction, and idiom. Some sentences are correct as is. No sentence has more than one error. You will find the error, if there is one, underlined and lettered. Elements of the sentence that are not underlined will not be changed. In choosing answers, follow the requirements of standard written English. If there is an error, select the one underlined part that must be changed to make the sentence correct. If there is no error, select choice **e**.

1. According to the reporter, there is multiple political reasons behind the unexpected riot
                a   **b**   **c**

going on downtown this afternoon. No error.
      d   **e**

2. Televisions, which have been a part of American culture for half a century, is more prevalent in American
                a   **b**   **c**

homes than functioning bathrooms. No error.
      d   **e**

3. Although various fans seen the winning shot clearly, the referee still would not change his initial ruling and
                  a   **b**   **c**

the player was instantly put on the bench. No error.
      d   **e**

4. At the local community library, patrons may check out an unlimited number of books, but the overdue
            a   **b**   **c**

fines are much higher than other libraries. No error.
      d   **e**

5. On the stage, the magician created an allusion that shocked the entire audience into total silence, followed
      a   **b**   **c**

by thundering applause. No error.
      d   **e**

6. Several award-winning authors publish only one book per year, but due to the ongoing media coverage,
            a   **b**   **c**

appeared to write much more. No error.
      d   **e**

7. A new homeowner commonly struggles to cope with a debt load that far exceeds their actual income.
      a   **b**   **c**   **d**
No error.
      e

8. One <u>cannot</u> get adequate physical rest <u>if you continuously</u> stay up too late, get up <u>too early</u>, and
              a   **b**   **c**
<u>skip meals too often</u>. <u>No error.</u>
        d   **e**

9. Studies <u>have shown</u> that the students who turn in <u>careful prepared</u> lab reports <u>do extremely well</u> in
              a   **b**   **c**
<u>science classes</u> such as chemistry and physics. <u>No error.</u>
     d   **e**

The following sentences test correctness and effectiveness of expression. In choosing answers, follow the requirements of standard written English; in other words, pay attention to grammar, choice of words, sentence construction, and punctuation. In each of the following sentences, part of the sentence or the entire sentence is underlined. Beneath each sentence, you will find five options for phrasing that underlined part. Choice **a** repeats the original, so if you believe it is correct as is, this is the correct answer. Your choice should produce the most effective sentence—clear and precise, without awkwardness or ambiguity.

10. While multiple movie makers try to convince filmgoers that global warming is just around the corner, <u>others, thanks to hard core research, not so sure.</u>
  a. others, thanks to hard core research, not so sure.
  b. others; thanks to hard core research; not so sure.
  c. others, thanks to hard core research, are not so sure.
  d. others thanks to hard core research so not so sure.
  e. others, thanks to hard core research, however, not so sure.

11. Sir Arthur Conan Doyle created one of the most well-known and admired detectives <u>in literature, Sherlock Holmes is recognized</u> in virtually every country of the world.
  a. in literature, Sherlock Holmes is recognized
  b. in literature Sherlock Holmes is recognized
  c. in literature; Sherlock Holmes is recognized
  d. in literature and Sherlock Holmes is recognized
  e. in literature, however, Sherlock Holmes is recognized

12. <u>The reluctant reporter asked the witnesses relevant questions from the local television station.</u>
  a. The reluctant reporter asked the witnesses relevant questions from the local television station.
  b. The reluctant reporter asked the witnesses relevant questions, from the local television station.
  c. From the local television station, witnesses were asked relevant questions by the reluctant reporter.
  d. The witnesses were asked relevant questions by the reluctant reporter since she was from the local television station.
  e. The reluctant reporter from the local television station asked the witnesses relevant questions.

13. The laptop computer was stored safely in the <u>luggage compartment; there was no chance</u> of it falling out or getting lost.
  a. luggage compartment; there was no chance
  b. luggage compartment, there was no chance
  c. luggage compartment because there was no chance
  d. luggage compartment; no chance
  e. luggage compartment there was no chance

14. <u>After studying for more than three hours, the test went much better than the student could have hoped.</u>
  a. After studying for more than three hours, the test went much better than the student could have hoped.
  b. Studying for more than three hours, the test went much better than the student could have hoped.
  c. The test went much better than the student could have ever hoped, he had studied for more than three hours.
  d. After studying for more than three hours, the student did much better on the test than he could have hoped.
  e. For more than three hours the student had studied, the test went much better than he could have hoped.

15. To qualify for the typical college scholarship, a student must <u>show financial need, have exemplary grades, or excelling</u> in some kind of sport.
  a. show financial need, have exemplary grades, or excelling
  b. show financial need, have exemplary grades, or excel
  c. show financial need, have exemplary grades, or excelled
  d. show financial need or have exemplary grades, or excelling
  e. show financial need, having exemplary grades, or excelling

16. Community libraries must continually strive for the necessary funds to purchase contemporary materials, <u>implement up-to-date technology, and continuously meeting</u> the varying needs of patrons.
  a. implement up-to-date technology, and continuously meeting
  b. implementing up-to-date technology, and continuously meeting
  c. implement up-to-date technology, and continuous meeting
  d. implementation of up-to-date technology, and continuously meeting
  e. implement up-to-date technology, and continuously meet

17. Charles Dickens wrote multiple best-selling novels in his <u>lifetime, because *A Christmas Carol* is the one the average person knows the best.</u>
  a. lifetime, because *A Christmas Carol* is the one the average person knows the best.
  b. lifetime, so *A Christmas Carol* is the one the average person knows the best.
  c. lifetime, but *A Christmas Carol* is the one the average person knows the best.
  d. lifetime, since *A Christmas Carol* is the one the average person knows the best.
  e. lifetime, *A Christmas Carol* is the one the average person knows the best.

18. Although she helped support each one of her brothers' grand endeavors, <u>but Orville and Wilbur Wright's sister Katherine was never truly perceived as a hero.</u>
  a. but Orville and Wilbur Wright's sister Katherine was never truly perceived as a hero.
  b. because Orville and Wilbur Wright's sister Katherine was never truly perceived as a hero.
  c. since Orville and Wilbur Wright's sister Katherine was never truly perceived as a hero.
  d. Orville and Wilbur Wright's sister Katherine was never truly perceived as a hero.
  e. and Orville and Wilbur Wright's sister Katherine was never truly perceived as a hero.

19. Since computers have become an integral part of modern American culture, <u>people of all ages and backgrounds have had to adapt to new terminology as well as new skills.</u>
  a. people of all ages and backgrounds have had to adapt to new terminology as well as new skills.
  b. because people of all ages and backgrounds have had to adapt to new terminology as well as new skills.
  c. although people of all ages and backgrounds have had to adapt to new terminology as well as new skills.
  d. however people of all ages and backgrounds have had to adapt to new terminology as well as new skills.
  e. for people of all ages and backgrounds have had to adapt to new terminology as well as new skills.

20. <u>Various famous writers have included nonsensical verse in their poetry,</u> no one has ever been able to do it as well as Lewis Carroll did in "Jabberwocky."
  a. Various famous writers have included nonsensical verse in their poetry,
  b. Although various famous writers have included nonsensical verse in their poetry,
  c. Because various famous writers have included nonsensical verse in their poetry,
  d. Since various famous writers have included nonsensical verse in their poetry,
  e. However, various famous writers have included nonsensical verse in their poetry,

21. Reality television is a trend that highlighted people's fascination with coping with common phobias, facing daunting challenges, <u>and win large amounts of money.</u>

   a. and win large amounts of money.
   b. plus win large amounts of money.
   c. and won large amounts of money.
   d. and large amounts of money.
   e. and winning large amounts of money.

The following passage is an early draft of a student's essay, and parts of it need to be rewritten. Read the passage and answer the questions that follow it. Some questions are about individual sentences or parts of sentences. Here, you are asked to select the choice that will improve the sentence structure and word choice. Other questions refer to parts of the essay or even the entire essay and ask you to look carefully at its organization and development. You should follow the conventions of standard written English in answering the questions.

(1) One of the most beautiful resources to inspire any young artist <u>can be found right outside your own front door.</u> (2) The world of nature offers limitless ideas for all the arts—from the beauty of a sunset and the lilting notes of birdsong to the graceful lines of an animal in motion or the starkness of tree limbs against a winter sky. (3) Many of the art's most famous masters turned to the world surrounding them to find the inspiration for their masterpieces.

(4) Children can easily become absorbed by nature's beauty. (5) Parents, usually wrapped up in maintaining the daily routine, may not recognize their children's fascination and hurry them along. (6) The cognizant parent can capitalize on these moments and show their children how the purity of a dandelion or the chattering of squirrels can be turned into anything from a sonnet to a sketch to a song.

(7) Best of all, souvenirs from nature are free, bountiful, and inspirational for children. (8) Leaves, flowers, seeds, weeds, acorns, bark, and twigs can be brought home and used to create collages, scrapbooks, poems, or ballads, thus preserving nature's beauty indefinitely.

22. In this essay, the author does all of the following EXCEPT

   a. explain how the world of nature can be a source of inspiration.
   b. give multiple, clear examples of ideas for art found in nature.
   c. provide precise directions on how to create a nature collage.
   d. describe how souvenirs from nature can be used for creativity.
   e. discuss how parents sometimes overlook artistic opportunities.

23. In context, which is the best revision of the underlined part of sentence 1 (reproduced below)?

One of the most beautiful resources to inspire any young artist <u>can be found right outside your own front door.</u>

   a. as it is now
   b. can be found right outside a child's own front door.
   c. can be found right outside their own front door.
   d. can be found right outside hers own front door.
   e. can be found right outside my own front door.

24. Which of the following is the best way to combine sentences 4 and 5 (reproduced below)?

Children can easily become absorbed by nature's beauty. Parents, usually wrapped up in maintaining the daily routine, may not recognize their children's fascination and hurry them along.

  a. Children can easily become absorbed by nature's beauty, but parents, usually wrapped up in maintaining the daily routine, may not recognize their children's fascination and hurry them along.
  b. Children can easily become absorbed by nature's beauty, parents, usually wrapped up in maintaining the daily routine, may not recognize their children's fascination and hurry them along.
  c. Children can easily become absorbed by nature's beauty because parents, usually wrapped up in maintaining the daily routine, may not recognize their children's fascination and hurry them along.
  d. Children can easily become absorbed by nature's beauty, furthermore, parents, usually wrapped up in maintaining the daily routine, may not recognize their children's fascination and hurry them along.
  e. Children can easily become absorbed by nature's beauty and parents, usually wrapped up in maintaining the daily routine, may not recognize their children's fascination and hurry them along.

25. *Some people believe that success comes through sheer drive and determination, while others think that it comes from natural and developed talents. Actress Sophia Loren once stated, "Getting ahead in a difficult profession requires avid faith in yourself. That is why some people with mediocre talent, but with great inner drive, go much further than people with vastly superior talent."*

  Assignment: What do you think is more important to success—talent or drive? Plan your response and write an essay in which you develop your point of view on this issue. Support your position with reasoning and examples taken from your reading, studies, experiences, or observations.

▶ Answers

1. b. In this question, the subject of the sentence (*reasons*) follows the verb (*is*). Plural subjects need plural verbs, so the sentence error is in choice **b**. Instead of *is*, the verb should be *are* in order to have subject-verb agreement.

2. c. In this question, the subject (*televisions*) has been separated from the verb (*is*) by a dependent clause (*which have been a part of American culture for half a century*). When you put them next to each other, you can see that the error is in **c**; it should read *are more prevalent.*

3. a. This question is testing your understanding of the past participle. In this example, the verb (*seen*) is a past participle and requires a helping verb (*have* or *be*). The way to correct choice **a** is to change *seen* to *saw.*

4. e. There is no error in this example. Remember that correct sentences will also be on the test.

5. b. At first glance, this sentence may seem correct. The error is in using the wrong word. It should not be *allusion*, which means to allude to something. It should be *illusion.*

6. d. There are two verbs in this sentence, and they must be in the same tense. The first verb (*publish*) is present, but the second one (*appeared*) is past. The error is in choice **d** where the verb should be changed to *appear.*

7. d. This is an example of using a pronoun in the wrong number. The subject (*homeowner*) is singular, and so the pronoun (*their*) should be singular also. It would be correct to say *far exceeds his or her actual income.*

8. b. This is an example of pronoun shift. The sentence begins with a noun (*one*) and then shifts to the wrong pronoun (*you*). When the noun *one* is used, he, she, one, or a person must follow it later.

9. b. This question is an example of a misuse of an adverb (*careful*). It is modifying the verb *prepared* and should have an *-ly* ending (*carefully*).

10. c. This is an example of a fragment. There is no verb in this sentence. Only choice **c** adds a verb (*are*) to make it a complete sentence. The other options add coordinating conjunctions, which does not repair the fragment.

11. c. This is an example of a run-on sentence. To repair it, you need to either insert a semicolon between the sentences or break them into two separate sentences. Choice **c** is the only one to do this.

12. e. This question tests your ability to spot a misplaced modifier. The phrase *from the local television station* modifies *reporter*, but because of its placement, it appears to modify *the witnesses*. It needs to be moved next to what it is supposed to modify, as shown in choice **e**. Choice **d** moves it closer but is wordy and redundant.

13. a. There is no error in this statement. It is an example of two complete sentences, which have been properly joined by a semicolon.

14. d. The way this is written, the test is what studied for three hours, instead of the student. The modifier needs to be placed next to what it is describing, as in choice **d**. Although it is moved in choice **e** as well, it is awkward and wordy.

15. b. This statement has an error called faulty parallelism. It has three verbs (*show*, *have*, and *excelling*), and they are not in the same tense. The way to correct this is to make *excelling* match the others, as in choice **b**.

16. e. This statement also has the error of faulty parallelism. There are four verbs (*strive*, *purchase*, *implement*, and *meeting*). The last one ends in *-ing*, and so it doesn't fit with the others. The correction is found in choice **e** where the last verb is changed to *meet.*

17. c. This type of question is testing whether or not you can recognize that you need to join two clauses correctly and show their relationship to each other. Here the two clauses (*Charles Dickens wrote multiple best-selling novels in his lifetime* and *A Christmas Carol is the one the average person knows the best*) are joined by *because*, but that does not show the correct relationship between the clauses. Instead, it should be *but*.

18. d. In this sentence, you have a dependent clause (*Although she helped support each one of her brothers' grand endeavors*), followed by another dependent clause (*but Orville and Wilbur Wright's sister Katherine was never truly perceived as a hero*). Whenever a sentence starts with a dependent clause (your clue is it cannot stand alone and starts with *although*), it must be followed by an independent clause (a statement that grammatically can stand on its own). If it doesn't, this is called faulty subordination. By removing the *but*, as in choice **d**, your second clause becomes dependent, and the sentence is correct.

19. a. There are no errors in this sentence. A dependent clause is followed by an independent one, and the statement is grammatically correct.

20. b. This question is testing you on recognizing a run-on sentence. Choice **b** turns the first sentence into a dependent clause, thus making the sentence correct.

21. e. This is another example of faulty parallelism. There are three verbs in the sentence (*coping*, *facing*, and *win*), and to be parallel, *win* needs to be changed to *winning*.

22. c. This question is looking at the essay's general organization or meaning. It wants to know if you understood what the author did—and did not do—in the essay. The essay did discuss how nature is a source of inspiration, where ideas can be found, what kind of souvenirs can be used, and how parents sometimes overlook opportunities. Although the essay did mention a collage, it did not provide directions on how to make one.

23. b. This is a question that focuses on revising or improving a sentence within the essay. In this example, the pronoun *your* is incorrect, as the rest of the essay is written in the third person. *Their* does not agree with *artist* because it is plural. *Hers* is a possessive pronoun and *my* is in the first person, so neither of these choices works, either. The only correct choice is **b**, which matches *child* to *artist*.

24. a. This question is asking you to combine two of the essay's sentences into one. This is a common SAT question. It is important that no meaning is lost and that the punctuation and grammar are correct in the answer choice you choose. It is also important that the right coordinating conjunction is used to fit the sentence's meaning. Choice **b** connects the sentences with a comma, creating a run-on sentence. Choices **c** and **d** use the wrong conjunction for the meaning of the sentence. Choice **e** adds *and*, which does not emphasize the correct meaning of the sentence.

25. Answers will vary.

CHAPTER

Ready, Get Set . . .

Taking a test is not necessarily a simple thing, especially when taking an influential one like the SAT. Most likely, your teachers, counselors, parents, and friends have told you repeatedly that the score you get on it is commonly a real factor in which colleges are willing to give you a chance and which ones are not.

lthough SAT scores are a long way from a life or death issue, they are unquestionably important. The key to getting high scores lies in adequate preparation, so let's get prepared.

▶ Keeping Calm, Cool, and Collected

If you have ever participated in any kind of competitive school activity like sports, debate, music, or drama, you know that it is normal to be nervous. Your hands could shake, you could sweat, and your breathing could be rapid. You are sure you have forgotten everything you have learned. You pace and wait as time slows down to a crawl. All of these are symptoms of anxiety, and whether you're getting ready to sing a solo or open your test booklet, they feel virtually the same.

Being nervous before you take the SAT is perfectly normal. A little anxiety can make you extra alert and even improve your performance. Too much anxiety can make you become virtually paralyzed. Obviously, the main way to avoid test anxiety is to be prepared for what is coming. That's simple; we will deal with that in the rest of the book. Here are some of the other ways to combat that mounting fear:

- **Get enough rest before the test.** You may think that staying up all night studying is going to improve your scores, but you're wrong. Fatigue will do more to lower your scores than any last-minute studying will raise it. Plan to get at least eight hours of sleep the night before the test and make them as restful as possible. No friends over, no late-night snacking sessions, and no distractions. Don't go overboard either and decide to sleep 14 or more hours straight either. That will just throw off your internal clock enough to have you completely confused by the time you go in to take the test.
- **Make sure you go into the test with a full stomach.** A good breakfast is essential. It will help keep you awake and alert, and you won't get distracted by those tummy rumbles. Avoid anything with caffeine, including chocolate, coffee, and soda. Caffeine may make you feel more awake, but it can increase the anxiety, and as it wears off, your energy may disappear completely.
- **Start off your test with some deep breathing.** In through the nose, out through the mouth to the count of at least ten. Do this several times. It will get your body to let go and relax a little bit more.
- **Stretch your neck and shoulders before you start.** Those muscles are the ones most likely to be carrying your stress as you take the test. If they can relax, then your body can concentrate on sending energy and blood flow to the most important part—your brain.
- **Think happy thoughts.** If you inundate your brain with negative thoughts like, *I'm going to flunk this test* or *This is going to go terribly*, then don't be too surprised when it happens. After all, you told you brain it was going to go badly, so it made sure that you were right. On the other hand, if you fill your mind with positive thoughts like *I will do well on this test* or *I am really prepared for the SAT*, then the same is true. Your mind will do its best to make sure this comes true for you as well.

It is very important to keep your test anxiety to a minimum. If you are focused on not throwing up or keeping your hands from shaking so much you can't hold the pencil, you certainly cannot concentrate on what the test is asking you to do. Practice deep breathing, stretching, and thinking positively for weeks before the test so you know how to call on these exercises for help on test day.

▶ A Valuable Strategy

The process of elimination (POE) is a great strategy when you are taking the SAT. Here are the basics: When you read a test question, two things will happen—either you will know the answer or you will not. If you know the answer right away, then mentally give yourself a pat on the back, fill in the appropriate little circle, and go on to the next question. If you do not know the answer, however, you will have to reread the question and choices.

For the first three parts of the SAT Writing section, you will be dealing with multiple-choice questions, and for each correct answer, you will receive one point. They are arranged in easy, medium, and hard levels. With multiple-choice questions, knowing how to use POE is quite important and helpful. You will have five answers to choose from. Scan them, and if you see one that you are sure is not the right one, get rid of it. Now you are down to four choices. Every time you can eliminate one answer choice, your chances of getting the answer right increase. If you get it down to four, it's a 25% chance of being right; down to three, it's 33.3%; down to two, it's 50%. When you keep in mind that a nonanswered question (left blank) is an automatic zero and you will only lose $\frac{1}{4}$ of a point for each wrong answer, you can see that taking out the answers you know are not correct and making an educated guess is a good strategy. Just remember, when you can narrow the choices, you have a better chance of getting the right answer.

▶ Time for an Overview

Now, let's take a detailed look at what goes into each type of question you will find on the SAT. Each one is unique and calls for a specific kind of response and knowledge. There are a total of 49 multiple-choice questions in the Writing section, and you will be given 35 minutes to complete them; that is more than one question a minute (just over 30 seconds each to be precise), so you have to keep moving.

Section 1: Identifying Sentence Errors Questions

This first section is going to see how well you can recognize a mistake in grammar or usage. It won't ask you to name or label it; you just have to recognize it and know the best way to fix it. Of course, here and there, the SAT will include a question that has no mistakes, and you need to be able to spot that question type as well. You will have approximately 18 questions on identifying sentence errors, so it is important to understand how they work.

With identifying sentence errors questions, always assume that the words and/or phrases that are NOT underlined are grammatically correct and that there is only one error.

Here is how one of these questions will look. A statement will have four parts (either words or phrases) underlined, and they will be labeled **a**, **b**, **c**, and **d**. Choice **e** will always be "No error," or in other words, the sentence is just fine as it is. Let's look at one:

<u>Even though</u> the number <u>of girls</u> coming to the party <u>are shrinking,</u> Katherine <u>is determined</u> to have it
     a   **b**   **c**   **d**
anyway. <u>No error.</u>
          e

Do any of the underlined words or phrases strike you as wrong? If so, great. You have your answer. If not, you need to reread.

Read the sentence aloud in your mind and see if you can "hear" a mistake. What answer did you come up with? If you choose **c**, you are right. The subject (*number*) is singular, so the verb should be also. This is an example of one of the most common questions on the SAT.

This section will test a lot of different grammar rules. The example you just read, for instance, tests subject-verb agreement. That is one of the 18 different things sentence errors will test you on. Here is the complete list. Please note that the ones with one asterisk (*) appear on the SAT an average of three times or more. Those with two asterisks (**) appear twice on average, and those with three asterisks (***) appear once on average.

1. subject-verb agreement when the subject follows the verb*
2. subject-verb agreement when the subject and verb are separated*
3. subject-verb agreement when the subject seems plural but is not*
4. confusion of the simple past and past participle*
5. confusion of the infinitive and gerund*
6. non-idiomatic preposition following a verb*
7. wrong word usage*
8. wrong verb tense*
9. number agreement problems**
10. pronoun in the wrong number**
11. pronoun in the wrong case in compound noun phrases**
12. pronoun shift**
13. pronoun with ambiguous reference**
14. faulty comparison***
15. misuse of adjective or adverb***
16. double negatives***
17. sentence fragments, run-ons, and comma splices***
18. parallel construction***

Don't be scared off by these names. Sometimes, people recognize these errors and how to fix them without knowing the exact grammar/usage rule that is being broken. Remember that you don't have to name the mistake or know the grammar rule; you just have to spot which underlined word or phrase is wrong and choose it.

> On average, about one in five questions in this section of the SAT is error-free (choice **e**). If you have fewer than this, you might be seeing mistakes where there aren't any. If you have a lot more, you are probably missing some errors.

Section 2: Improving Sentences Questions

This section is similar to the first one; the main difference is how you are choosing an answer. Instead of pointing out the word or phrase that is wrong and being done with it, here you will be figuring out if something is wrong with one underlined word or phrase and picking the best version of the underlined portion of the sentence. You will have approximately 25 of this type of question to answer in this section of the SAT.

With improving sentences questions, answer choice **a** will always be a repeat of the underlined portion. If you choose **a**, it means you are saying there is no error.

Here is how one of these questions will look:

The Civil Rights Movement fought to show everyone that all people are <u>created equal this is a right</u> set forth in the Declaration of Independence.

a. created equal this is a right
b. created equal, this is a right
c. created equal; since this is a right
d. created equal; this is a right
e. created equality; this is a right

Did you spot an error? Clearly, this is a question dealing with proper punctuation. Which one fixes the error, or is there an error? In this case, the correct answer is **d**. This is a run-on sentence, and it can be repaired by either inserting a semicolon, a period, or a coordinating conjunction. Choice **d** was the only one to do this.

In this portion of the test, you will be tested on errors in grammar, expression, or style. Examples will include mistakes in word choice, sentence structure, grammar, usage, and punctuation. You will need to know how to identify:

1. run-on sentences
2. fragments
3. misplaced modifiers
4. faulty parallelism
5. faulty coordination or subordination

The process of elimination works especially well in this portion of the test. Immediately strike out the ones that you know are wrong and see what you are left with. As a general rule, never choose an answer that substantially changes the meaning of the entire sentence, even if it is grammatically correct.

Section 3: Improving Paragraphs Questions

This section has fewer questions than the others (approximately 6), but that's good because they take a lot more time to answer. The reason is simple: You have a lot more to read for each one.

In this section, you will have what looks like a student's first draft of a paper, usually ranging between three and five paragraphs long. You will be asked multiple questions about each essay. These questions might involve a single sentence in the essay, or they could cover phrases, paragraphs, or the entire essay. Each sentence will be numbered for easy reference back to it. The most common things you will be asked to do are: *revise* (relocate, remove, or add a sentence; or fix an error as in the second section of the test where you are asked to pick the best version of the underlined portion of the sentence), *combine* (put two or more sentences together in order to show proper coordination or subordination), and answer questions about *content* (describe the purpose of or find the main idea of a particular paragraph).

Here are some examples of this type of question:

(1) Going on the road and keeping up with your e-mail can be quite the challenge for some travelers. (2) If you can afford to stay in the expensive hotels that either offer free or relatively inexpensive Internet service, it may not be much of an issue. (3) However, many travelers do not have that option, including those who are renting cabins, pitching tents, or have to stay in budget motels. (4) What choices do they have?

(5) For these journeyers, it may come down to using public libraries, visiting coffee shops, or searching billboards for those magical words *Internet service available*. (6) None of these options is terribly convenient, and some of them can end up being more than a little spendy. (7) Others are really time-consuming.

(8) Finding a place to get access to the Internet is often difficult. (9) You are frequently in an unfamiliar city with little to no idea where to find anything beyond a gas station and a fast-food restaurant. (10) If you happen to have your own laptop, of course, you can just search for a place offering free wifi. (11) That is the way the future is going.

In context, which of the following is the best way to revise sentence 3?

However, many travelers do not have that option, including those who are renting cabins, pitching tents, or have to stay in budget motels.

a. as it is now
b. However, many travelers do not have that option, including those who are rent cabins, pitch tents, or stay in budget motels.
c. However, many travelers do not have that option, including those who are renting cabins, pitching tents, or staying in budget motels.
d. However, many travelers do not have that option, including renting cabins, pitching tents, or staying in budget motels.
e. However, many travelers do not have the option of renting cabins, pitching tents, or staying in budget motels.

This question is focusing on one particular sentence in the essay. Did you spot the mistake? This time it happens to be in parallelism. The verbs *rent*, *pitch*, and *stay* should all be parallel. Choice **c** makes them parallel (all end in -*ing*) without changing the meaning of the sentence.

What is the best way to combine sentences 6 and 7?

None of these options is terribly convenient, and some of them can end up being more than a little spendy. Others are really time-consuming.

a. None of these options is terribly convenient, and some of them can end up being more than a little spendy; time-consuming.
b. None of these options is terribly convenient, and some of them can end up more than a little spendy, others are really time-consuming.
c. None of these options is terribly convenient, and some of them can end up being more than a little spendy because they are really time-consuming.
d. None of these options is terribly convenient, and some of them can end up being more than a little spendy, and others are really very time-consuming.
e. None of these options is terribly convenient, and some of them can end up being more than a little spendy and time-consuming.

This question is asking you about several sentences within the essay. Which one of these options best combines the information and retains the original meaning without creating a grammatical error? If you chose **e**, you are correct. It eliminated wordiness and used correct punctuation.

Here is one more question about the same essay.

The writer's main purpose of the essay is to
a. prove that getting your e-mail on the road is impossible.
b. persuade readers to get their own laptops before traveling.
c. show how more expensive hotels are the better option to use.
d. describe the different options travelers have to get their e-mail.
e. analyze the most inexpensive way to track down wifi in a town.

This question is asking you about the essay as a whole. Which one do you think best summarizes the main idea of the essay? If you chose **d**, you are correct. This essay does not say getting e-mail is impossible, nor does it try to persuade readers or analyze wifi trends.

Other questions that could be asked about this essay include improving content by providing more details or examples (Why is a place inconvenient? How much is expensive? Why do some places take up so much time? Why does having your own laptop make a difference?), whether *spendy* is a word that should be used in a formal essay, and whether the essay could be improved by removing the last sentence.

In this section, you will generally be tested on spotting:

1. flaws in organization
2. faulty emphasis on ideas
3. illogical development
4. disjointed thinking
5. errors in basic grammar, usage, and style

With this type of question, it is important that you read the entire essay, but read it quickly so that you get the gist of it without the details. Once you start answering the questions, you can go back and read which section you need to make the right choice. Be sure to read the sentence before and after the section you are being asked about because it is often relevant to determining the correct answer.

Section 4: Responding to Writing Prompts

Okay, the multiple-choice portion is now over. Take another one of those deep breaths because it is time to start the newest part of the SAT: the essay. You will have 25 minutes to read the prompt, respond, and write your essay, so you need to know what to expect.

Here is the good news. First of all, you are not being graded on punctuation or spelling in this essay. However, while the scorers will not be checking your spelling or making sure there are no comma splices, if you have enough of these kinds of mistakes, it will make your essay harder to read and understand. If this happens, your score is bound to reflect it. Secondly, you will be given a topic, so you don't have to come up with one of your own.

Sigh again. Lastly, accuracy isn't necessary either. If you botch a date or a name, don't worry about it. It won't factor into your score.

Now for the tough stuff. You will primarily be expected to write in complete sentences and without using a great deal of slang. You will have about 240 lines to fill up and you need to *fill them up*. That usually works out to be between 300 and 450 words, depending on your handwriting. Don't try to write big, skip lines, or make huge indentations for each paragraph. You need to fill those lines up with the best thesis statement and supporting details that you can possibly come up with in your limited time slot. Fill them up. Don't go over and don't leave more than a couple blank (at most). Lastly, make your writing legible. In this day of doing everything on the computer, it may feel very strange to handwrite a paper, but until they implement online SATs, you have to handwrite your essay. If it is impossible or just challenging to read, can you imagine how the SAT test scorer is going to react when he or she sees it? Don't hurt your score just because you scribble.

The essay portion of the SAT is designed to give you a writing prompt that you read and respond to with your own personal opinion, experiences, and/or knowledge. There is no right or wrong answer; if you want to say that yes, you think Barry Manilow was the best songwriter of the twentieth century, or that no, making dyed hair illegal is not a good idea, that's fine. The scorers are not here to tell you your opinions are correct or incorrect. They just want to see how well you write and support them.

Your writing prompt will consist either of a quote or a paragraph that you need to respond to. Here is an example of each kind:

It has often been said that our actions speak louder than our words. As John Ruskin once stated, "What we think, or what we know, or what we believe, is in the end, of little consequence. The only thing of consequence is what we do."

Assignment: What truly defines a person's character the most: words or actions? Plan your response and support your position with specific points and examples from your observations, studies, reading, or personal experiences.

Some cities in the United States have set up curfews for anyone under the age of 18. Although some have reported positive changes in crime rates and other issues, others have not seen any significant improvements.

Assignment: Does putting legal restrictions on young people help them stay safer or make them feel confined? Plan your response and support your position with specific points and examples from your observations, studies, reading, or personal experiences.

In both kinds of prompts, the key is to read and understand what is being asked and then respond with a definite opinion and supporting details. Make sure that you clearly understand what you are being asked to write about. The only way you are going to get a zero on your essay is to leave it blank, write it illegibly, or write on the wrong subject.

Your essay will be graded on the following:

1. Did you address the correct topic?
2. Did you state an opinion one way or another?
3. Did you organize your points in a logical manner?
4. Did you have supporting details for the main point?
5. Were your details specific and detailed?

Although spelling and punctuation are not graded, they can affect the paper holistically, so do your best to make sure these elements are correct. Of course, if you can remember to include some great paragraph transitions, a strong introduction and conclusion, and several strong examples for the body, your chance of a high score is much better.

Ideally, after you read your writing prompt, you will take the time to roughly outline and/or brainstorm what you want to say in your response. Time is limited, however, so that may prove impossible for you. Here is some good advice on managing your time:

Minutes 0 to 5	Read and understand the prompt; then form your response.
Minutes 6 to 20	Write the essay from beginning to end.
Minutes 21 to 25	Proof for any mistakes and correct them.

▶ What's the Score?

On the multiple-choice portion of the test, you get one point for each correct answer, a quarter of a point off for each incorrect answer, and no points for blank or unanswered questions. That is pretty cut and dried. It is a little less so on the essays.

On the essay, scores range from 0 to 6 points. Two scorers (usually a high school English teacher or a college English teacher) will read your essay, and each one of them will give it a score. They usually read through it once as a whole and then score it. If the two graders' scores are more than one point apart (i.e. one gives your essay a 4, while another gives it a 2 or 6), a third scorer reads it and determines the final score.

Now that you know what to expect in the SAT Writing section, let's put those theories into practice. Sharpen your pencils and get ready for practice, practice, practice.

CHAPTER

2

Recognizing Sentence Errors

The following are examples of the different identifying sentence errors questions that you will be tested on in the SAT. There are 114 practice questions, which means that you will know these types of questions backward, forward, and upside down!

RECOGNIZING SENTENCE ERRORS

1.	(a) (b) (c) (d) (e)	41.	(a) (b) (c) (d) (e)	81.	(a) (b) (c) (d) (e)
2.	(a) (b) (c) (d) (e)	42.	(a) (b) (c) (d) (e)	82.	(a) (b) (c) (d) (e)
3.	(a) (b) (c) (d) (e)	43.	(a) (b) (c) (d) (e)	83.	(a) (b) (c) (d) (e)
4.	(a) (b) (c) (d) (e)	44.	(a) (b) (c) (d) (e)	84.	(a) (b) (c) (d) (e)
5.	(a) (b) (c) (d) (e)	45.	(a) (b) (c) (d) (e)	85.	(a) (b) (c) (d) (e)
6.	(a) (b) (c) (d) (e)	46.	(a) (b) (c) (d) (e)	86.	(a) (b) (c) (d) (e)
7.	(a) (b) (c) (d) (e)	47.	(a) (b) (c) (d) (e)	87.	(a) (b) (c) (d) (e)
8.	(a) (b) (c) (d) (e)	48.	(a) (b) (c) (d) (e)	88.	(a) (b) (c) (d) (e)
9.	(a) (b) (c) (d) (e)	49.	(a) (b) (c) (d) (e)	89.	(a) (b) (c) (d) (e)
10.	(a) (b) (c) (d) (e)	50.	(a) (b) (c) (d) (e)	90.	(a) (b) (c) (d) (e)
11.	(a) (b) (c) (d) (e)	51.	(a) (b) (c) (d) (e)	91.	(a) (b) (c) (d) (e)
12.	(a) (b) (c) (d) (e)	52.	(a) (b) (c) (d) (e)	92.	(a) (b) (c) (d) (e)
13.	(a) (b) (c) (d) (e)	53.	(a) (b) (c) (d) (e)	93.	(a) (b) (c) (d) (e)
14.	(a) (b) (c) (d) (e)	54.	(a) (b) (c) (d) (e)	94.	(a) (b) (c) (d) (e)
15.	(a) (b) (c) (d) (e)	55.	(a) (b) (c) (d) (e)	95.	(a) (b) (c) (d) (e)
16.	(a) (b) (c) (d) (e)	56.	(a) (b) (c) (d) (e)	96.	(a) (b) (c) (d) (e)
17.	(a) (b) (c) (d) (e)	57.	(a) (b) (c) (d) (e)	97.	(a) (b) (c) (d) (e)
18.	(a) (b) (c) (d) (e)	58.	(a) (b) (c) (d) (e)	98.	(a) (b) (c) (d) (e)
19.	(a) (b) (c) (d) (e)	59.	(a) (b) (c) (d) (e)	99.	(a) (b) (c) (d) (e)
20.	(a) (b) (c) (d) (e)	60.	(a) (b) (c) (d) (e)	100.	(a) (b) (c) (d) (e)
21.	(a) (b) (c) (d) (e)	61.	(a) (b) (c) (d) (e)	101.	(a) (b) (c) (d) (e)
22.	(a) (b) (c) (d) (e)	62.	(a) (b) (c) (d) (e)	102.	(a) (b) (c) (d) (e)
23.	(a) (b) (c) (d) (e)	63.	(a) (b) (c) (d) (e)	103.	(a) (b) (c) (d) (e)
24.	(a) (b) (c) (d) (e)	64.	(a) (b) (c) (d) (e)	104.	(a) (b) (c) (d) (e)
25.	(a) (b) (c) (d) (e)	65.	(a) (b) (c) (d) (e)	105.	(a) (b) (c) (d) (e)
26.	(a) (b) (c) (d) (e)	66.	(a) (b) (c) (d) (e)	106.	(a) (b) (c) (d) (e)
27.	(a) (b) (c) (d) (e)	67.	(a) (b) (c) (d) (e)	107.	(a) (b) (c) (d) (e)
28.	(a) (b) (c) (d) (e)	68.	(a) (b) (c) (d) (e)	108.	(a) (b) (c) (d) (e)
29.	(a) (b) (c) (d) (e)	69.	(a) (b) (c) (d) (e)	109.	(a) (b) (c) (d) (e)
30.	(a) (b) (c) (d) (e)	70.	(a) (b) (c) (d) (e)	110.	(a) (b) (c) (d) (e)
31.	(a) (b) (c) (d) (e)	71.	(a) (b) (c) (d) (e)	111.	(a) (b) (c) (d) (e)
32.	(a) (b) (c) (d) (e)	72.	(a) (b) (c) (d) (e)	112.	(a) (b) (c) (d) (e)
33.	(a) (b) (c) (d) (e)	73.	(a) (b) (c) (d) (e)	113.	(a) (b) (c) (d) (e)
34.	(a) (b) (c) (d) (e)	74.	(a) (b) (c) (d) (e)	114.	(a) (b) (c) (d) (e)
35.	(a) (b) (c) (d) (e)	75.	(a) (b) (c) (d) (e)		
36.	(a) (b) (c) (d) (e)	76.	(a) (b) (c) (d) (e)		
37.	(a) (b) (c) (d) (e)	77.	(a) (b) (c) (d) (e)		
38.	(a) (b) (c) (d) (e)	78.	(a) (b) (c) (d) (e)		
39.	(a) (b) (c) (d) (e)	79.	(a) (b) (c) (d) (e)		
40.	(a) (b) (c) (d) (e)	80.	(a) (b) (c) (d) (e)		

▶ Questions

1. In Pacific Northwest <u>cities</u> like Seattle and Portland, there <u>isn't</u> hardly a <u>single day</u> when <u>no rain</u> falls.
                                  a   **b**   **c**   **d**
<u>No error.</u>
    e

2. Of the two digital cameras he <u>showed</u> me, I liked the silver one <u>the best</u>, <u>not only</u> because of its high pixels,
                                a   **b**   **c**
but also because of <u>its</u> price. <u>No error.</u>
            d   **e**

3. If you plan on missing more than two basketball practices, you <u>should contact</u> your coach <u>directly</u>, or if you
                                                      a   **b**
cannot reach him, <u>one must call</u> the school administration office as soon as <u>possible</u>. <u>No error.</u>
             c   **d**   **e**

4. The <u>gathering</u> of dark storm clouds, <u>clearly indicated</u> on the weatherman's map, <u>were</u> <u>definitely</u> indicative
       a   **b**   **c**   **d**
of an upcoming major weather event. <u>No error.</u>
                            e

5. Much to the <u>dismay and disappointment</u> of thousands of fans, <u>neither</u> the "Buffy, the Vampire Slayer" <u>nor</u>
                    a   **b**   **c**
"Angel" series is going <u>to be renewed</u> for television. <u>No error.</u>
                    d   **e**

6. The telephone rang <u>so</u> <u>unexpected</u> and there was such chaos already going on in the dorm room that it
                        a   **b**
was <u>virtually</u> impossible to hear who was <u>speaking</u> on the other end. <u>No error.</u>
         c   **d**   **e**

7. <u>To write</u> a research paper <u>good</u>, you must <u>not only understand</u> the basics of grammar, spelling, and
    a   **b**   **c**
punctuation, you must also be able to tell the difference between reliable facts and <u>someone's</u> personal
                                                                                   d
opinion. <u>No error.</u>
            e

8. <u>All year round</u>, tourists <u>come</u> to Oregon <u>to hike</u> the tree-covered hills, explore the pine forests, ski on the
     a   b   c

snowy mountains, visit the sandy coast, and <u>swimming in the chilly ocean</u>. <u>No error</u>.
                                     d   e

9. If one truly appreciates movies with <u>unbelievable and unexpected</u> twists, <u>you</u> certainly have to see
                                  a   b

<u>every single movie</u> M. Night Shyamalan has ever <u>produced</u>. <u>No error</u>.
     c   d   e

10. Horror <u>writers</u>, such as Stephen King, Dean Koontz, Clive Barker, and John Saul, <u>commonly appears</u> at
      a   b

national conventions where <u>they</u> meet with fans, <u>sign their books</u>, and speak to crowds. <u>No error</u>.
                          c   d   e

11. The <u>cost</u> of first-class postage stamps continues <u>to rise</u> every <u>few years, however</u>, the price is still
      a   b   c

<u>relatively miniscule</u> considering how far one stamp can take an envelope. <u>No error</u>.
     d   e

12. When Caroline <u>opened</u> the front door of her apartment, the guests and all the family members
                 a

<u>that had come</u> from near and far jumped up from <u>his or her</u> hiding place and <u>shouted</u>, "Surprise!" <u>No error</u>.
     b   c   d   e

13. Although <u>volunteering looks good</u> on a resume and can increase a <u>high school student's</u> chance of
                   a   b

obtaining a scholarship, <u>they</u> take other elements into <u>consideration</u>, including grades, test scores, and
                            c   d

financial background. <u>No error</u>.
                   e

14. Neither of the contestants <u>are</u> planning <u>to pursue</u> a career in entertainment after their <u>dismal failure</u> in
                           a   b   c

front of the judges of *American Idol* even though <u>they</u> still wanted to be performers. <u>No error</u>.
                                           d   e

15. The second haunted house was definitely the <u>scariest</u> of the two, <u>although</u> it was not quite as dark inside
                                    a   b

and had <u>a lot less</u> small, <u>screaming children</u> running through it. <u>No error</u>.
            c   d   e

16. Flightless birds, such as ostriches and emus, retain <u>their wings</u>, which they <u>primarily use</u> for balance when
ab

<u>they run, they</u> even have been known to flap their wings up and down in order <u>to maintain</u> a comfortable
cd

temperature. <u>No error.</u>
e

17. <u>Although</u> castles were <u>commonly cold</u> and uncomfortable places<u>, they</u> were <u>cunningly designed</u> to
abcd

withstand the siege of enemy forces, thanks to small windows, stone walls, and protective towers. <u>No error.</u>
e

18. The naïve first-year <u>college student</u> <u>frequently</u> sleeps too late and parties too much, which, not too
ab

<u>surprisingly</u>, can lead to <u>their failing</u> a class or even losing a scholarship. <u>No error.</u>
cde

19. Joseph's <u>weekend plans</u> so far included finishing his research paper, paying his rent and <u>utilities</u>, stopping
ab

in for a visit with <u>his grandparents</u>, and <u>to make out</u> a new class schedule. <u>No error.</u>
cde

20. When we were <u>lined up</u> in front of the concert hall yesterday, Shasta, the new girl I told you about from
a

Mr. Henry's <u>science class</u>, was the one <u>standing</u> between <u>you and I</u>. <u>No error.</u>
bcde

21. <u>Although</u> the fire department is currently calling for additional volunteers to help fight the local fires,
a

<u>they</u> do not seem to be getting a response from the <u>vast majority</u> of <u>townspeople</u>. <u>No error.</u>
bcde

22. The co-ed, <u>newly formed</u> basketball team, sponsored by several local organizations and <u>businesses</u>,
ab

<u>were already dressed</u> in brand-new uniforms <u>and ready</u> to hit the court. <u>No error.</u>
cde

23. Each of the authors <u>who was honored</u> at the city's new bookstore's open house <u>had been writing</u> for more
ab

than 20 years and <u>had published</u> at least two national best-sellers during <u>his or her</u> career. <u>No error.</u>
cde

24. The medical study revealed that <u>patients who</u> asked their physicians questions <u>during the consultation</u>
                                          a   **b**
responded better to treatment <u>than</u> those who <u>are quiet</u> throughout the appointment. <u>No error.</u>
                      c   **d**   **e**

25. It has been thought for <u>many years</u> that three-fourths of the planet Earth <u>was</u> covered in water, but in
                              a   **b**
recent years, some <u>experts</u> have begun to <u>suspect</u> that it might be even more than that. <u>No error.</u>
                    c   **d**   **e**

26. According to the <u>teacher's tally</u> of votes, more than 60% of the <u>history class</u> <u>are interested</u> in taking a field
                                a   **b**   **c**
trip <u>to tour</u> the new art museum downtown. <u>No error.</u>
   d   **e**

27. <u>According</u> to the newspaper survey, <u>neither</u> of the proposed candidates actually <u>have</u> enough experience or
   a   **b**   **c**
education to mount a <u>truly</u> impressive or successful campaign. <u>No error.</u>
                    d   **e**

28. The <u>bulk</u> of Lewis Carroll's stories, as well as <u>his</u> famous poems like "The Jabberwocky," <u>are</u> full of
      a   **b**   **c**
nonsense terms that <u>are confusing</u> and amusing at the same time. <u>No error.</u>
                  d   **e**

29. <u>Behind</u> the stage <u>were</u> the props, dressing rooms, rack of costumes, and <u>a place</u> for all of the actors and
   a   **b**   **c**
actresses <u>to relax and rest</u> between acts. <u>No error.</u>
            d   **e**

30. <u>Everybody</u> <u>who</u> shows up to help with the float for the parade <u>is</u> going to receive unlimited pizza, soda, and
   a   **b**   **c**
cookies, <u>as well as</u> a special community volunteering badge. <u>No error.</u>
          d   **e**

31. <u>Anyone</u> interested in joining the <u>newly</u> formed drama club that <u>meets on Friday</u> afternoons <u>are</u> welcome to
   a   **b**   **c**   **d**
attend an orientation meeting this week from 4:00 P.M. to 6:00 P.M. <u>No error.</u>
                                                  e

32. In most public libraries <u>throughout the community</u>, there <u>isn't</u> hardly a single book, magazine, video, or
                                                    a   **b**

    <u>compact disc</u> that has not been <u>checked</u> out at least a dozen times. <u>No error.</u>
      c   **d**   **e**

33. Without a doubt, Kevin <u>is the best runner</u> on the team <u>because</u> his speed, stamina, and stride <u>guarantees</u> a
                              a   **b**   **c**

    strong performance <u>in every single event</u> he participates in. <u>No error.</u>
                        d   **e**

34. The ten-foot-tall arbor vitae hedges <u>on either side</u> of our house <u>provide</u> an immense amount of <u>shade</u> in
                                      a   **b**   **c**

    the summertime and <u>welcome protection</u> from the wind during the winter. <u>No error.</u>
                    d   **e**

35. When I first <u>joined</u> the high school debate club, the senior team <u>leaders were</u> <u>unbelievably</u> strict about
             a   **b**   **c**

    making you attend every single practice and have <u>one's parents</u> go to all competitive events. <u>No error.</u>
                                    d   **e**

36. Considering the extreme heat today, I <u>think</u> it would be rather <u>inadvisable</u> for you to <u>ride</u> your bicycle as
                                    a   **b**   **c**

    <u>quick</u> as you did. <u>No error.</u>
    d   **e**

37. Numerous Super Bowl fans <u>thoroughly</u> enjoy watching both teams' cheerleaders, <u>firmly</u> believing that <u>they</u>
                            a   **b**   **c**

    are the most <u>entertaining aspect</u> of the entire experience. <u>No error.</u>
                  d   **e**

38. After the tree was cut down, the <u>workers spent</u> the next few hours <u>cutting</u> off the numerous branches,
                                a   **b**

    <u>sweeping</u> up the debris, and <u>pick up</u> the piles of leaves left on the ground. <u>No error.</u>
      c   **d**   **e**

39. To mow a yard <u>good</u>, you must make sure the lawn mower <u>is always kept</u> in reliable condition and <u>verify</u> if
                a   **b**   **c**

    the homeowner <u>has any specific</u> landscaping requests or parameters. <u>No error.</u>
                    d   **e**

40. <u>At the beginning</u> of the movie, my friend Richard <u>quietly moved</u> into the empty seat between <u>my sister and I</u>
　　　　　a　　　　　　　　　　　　　　　　　　b　　　　　　　　　　　　　　　　　　　　c

so that he could see the screen <u>better</u>. <u>No error.</u>
　　　　　　　　　　　　　　　　　　　　d　　　　e

41. At the end of the evening, the class president, secretary, and treasurer all <u>sweared</u> that <u>they</u> would take
　　　　　　　　　　　　　　　　　　　　　　　　　　　　　　　　　　　　　　　a　　　　　b

their jobs <u>seriously</u> and uphold all of the inherent responsibilities that came with <u>these important positions</u>.
　　　　　　　c　　　　　　　　　　　　　　　　　　　　　　　　　　　　　　　　　　　d

<u>No error.</u>
　　e

42. Nicole <u>could hardly</u> do <u>no</u> better than to have taken <u>first place</u> in the Dance, Dance Revolution contest at
　　　　　　　a　　　　　　b　　　　　　　　　　　　c

the local <u>game store</u>. <u>No error.</u>
　　　　　　d　　　　　e

43. Before she <u>enrolled</u> in community college, an attitude of apathy and lethargy <u>were</u> common, and thoughts
　　　　　　　a　　　　　　　　　　　　　　　　　　　　　　　　　　　　　b

about the future <u>were</u> <u>rarely</u> ever considered. <u>No error.</u>
　　　　　　　　　c　　　d　　　　　　　　　　e

44. The second feature was definitely the <u>longest</u> of the two movies, <u>although</u> it was so riveting and had such
　　　　　　　　　　　　　　　　　a　　　　　　　　　　　b

amazing special effects that I <u>hardly</u> even <u>noticed</u>. <u>No error.</u>
　　　　　　　　　　　　　c　　　　　d　　　　e

45. Right before the new school year <u>started</u>, the classroom, like many of the others in the school,
　　　　　　　　　　　　　　　　　a

<u>had been repainted</u> and cleaned, while the desks were <u>polished</u> and <u>rearranged</u>. <u>No error.</u>
　　b　　　　　　　　　　　　　　　　　　　　c　　　　　　d　　　　　e

46. Michelle's postcards, ticket stubs, magazine clippings, and personal letters <u>were glued</u> into her new
　　　　　　　　　　　　　　　　　　　　　　　　　　　　　　　　　　　　　a

scrapbook; <u>they</u> represented the diversity and excitement that <u>defines</u> her <u>life</u> and personality. <u>No error.</u>
　　　　　　b　　　　　　　　　　　　　　　　　　　c　　　d　　　　　　　　　　e

47. As the producer stated in the DVD's extras, to <u>represent</u> the tragedy of AIDS in Africa and how it has
　　　　　　　　　　　　　　　　　　　　　a

<u>destroyed</u> the lives of thousands was the entire point of <u>him</u> <u>producing</u> the movie. <u>No error.</u>
　　b　　　　　　　　　　　　　　　　　　　c　　　d　　　　　　　　e

48. <u>At</u> which point during the wedding ceremony <u>does</u> the <u>people</u> in the church stand up and repeat the verses
    a   b   c

<u>after</u> the minister? <u>No error.</u>
  d   e

49. My parents can't <u>understand</u> my television preferences, such as *Bones*, *CSI*, *Night Stalker*, or *Medium*
                      a

<u>because</u> <u>they</u> think <u>it</u> is too unsettling and disturbing. <u>No error.</u>
  b   c   d   e

50. Of the two Clive Cussler novels I have read, I like *Inca Gold* <u>the best</u>, not only because I <u>liked</u> that era in
                                                 a   b

history, <u>but also</u> because of <u>its</u> gutsy main character, Dirk Pitt. <u>No error.</u>
     c   d   e

51. For <u>as long as</u> I can remember, my two brothers and I <u>fighted</u> about almost every possible topic, <u>including</u>
      a   b   c

what day it was, who was <u>taller</u>, and why the Beatles broke up. <u>No error.</u>
                  d   e

52. A number of the teachers <u>which</u> were <u>working</u> at the local community college were found <u>to have attended</u>
                      a   b   c

the exact same college and <u>even graduated</u> the very same year. <u>No error.</u>
                    d   e

53. If you are going <u>to support</u> the idea of Lyssa starting her own thrift shop, you should start gathering your
                  a

<u>family's</u> donations, and <u>when one</u> has at least three large garbage bags full of stuff, take it all over so she can
    b   c

start <u>pricing</u> everything. <u>No error.</u>
     d   e

54. The group of skaters <u>which</u> was practicing <u>daily</u> in the hopes of qualifying for the Olympics <u>was</u> found to
                   a   b   c

be skipping school on a regular basis in order <u>to fit in</u> more hours out on the rink. <u>No error.</u>
                               d   e

55. Many cell phone <u>companies offer</u> flexible programs like rollover minutes, family plans, and music
                    a

downloads because <u>they</u> think that <u>will</u> win over a growing number of new <u>customers</u>. <u>No error.</u>
        b   c   d   e

56. When Jasmine <u>set out</u> to find a job, she decided that <u>she would start</u> with businesses <u>different than</u> the ones
                         a   b   c

her friends went to, <u>including</u> the bookstore, candy shop, and coffee bistro. <u>No error.</u>
                  d   e

57. The riveting *The Da Vinci Code* by Dan Brown <u>has been read</u> by more people than <u>any other</u> in the
                                                a   b

<u>long history</u> of *The New York Times* <u>national</u> best-sellers lists. <u>No error.</u>
    c   d   e

58. If one <u>takes</u> the time to plan a vacation, map the best route, reserve the hotels, purchase the tickets, <u>and</u>
        a   b

pack the luggage, the least <u>you</u> could do <u>is</u> be ready on time! <u>No error.</u>
                         c   d   e

59. <u>Although</u> Lydia knows everything there is to know about trees and plants, <u>they</u> do not think that <u>her</u> idea
        a   b   c

of <u>opening</u> her own nursery is a very good one. <u>No error.</u>
      d   e

60. <u>After</u> the whole terrible incident was <u>finally</u> over, I <u>shaked</u> from my head to my toes and I <u>was covered</u> in
        a   b   c   d

goose bumps. <u>No error.</u>
                   e

61. Of the two Alfred Hitchcock movies I <u>have seen</u>, I like *Psycho* <u>the best</u>, not only because of its lighting,
                                           a   b

<u>but also</u> because Anthony Perkins <u>is</u> one of my favorite actors. <u>No error.</u>
    c   d   e

62. She and <u>I</u> earned enough money from the recyclables we <u>turned</u> in at the community center to have
          a   b

enough <u>to get</u> both of the compact discs that <u>we</u> wanted. <u>No error.</u>
          c   d   e

63. In large bookstores <u>like</u> Borders and Barnes and Noble, there <u>isn't</u> hardly a single plush chair <u>where</u> <u>no</u>
                              a   b   c   d

people are sitting, browsing through books, or paging through magazines. <u>No error.</u>
                                                                 e

64. If he <u>truly</u> enjoys action and adventure movies, <u>I</u> will <u>certainly</u> enjoy <u>watching</u> anything starring Jean
      a   **b**   **c**   **d**
Claude van Damme, Steven Seagal, Chuck Norris, Jackie Chan, or Jet Li. <u>No error.</u>
                                                                      e

65. Birds <u>like</u> swifts and swallows spend the majority of the year living in central and <u>southern Africa;</u> in the
         a   **b**
dry season, however, <u>they fly</u> to Europe where there <u>is</u> more food and warmer climates. <u>No error.</u>
                            c   **d**   **e**

66. Although Alexander Graham Bell <u>was</u> the one who discovered how to send the human voice along wires,
                                            a
<u>but</u> it was Guglielmo Marconi <u>who</u> built the first machine able <u>to send</u> messages by radio wave. <u>No error.</u>
b   **c**   **d**   **e**

67. A good radio disc jockey is <u>someone</u> <u>who</u> plays the right combination of popular songs and golden oldies,
                                a   **b**
talks directly and <u>personally</u> to the listeners, and inserts commercials where needed. Also, <u>their</u> voice
                          c   **d**
should be deep and soothing. <u>No error.</u>
                              e

68. In the Shakespearian play, the character of Macbeth, a man with a <u>domineering</u> wife and a weak will, is
                                                    a
going <u>to kill</u> the king so he can take his place, but in the end, Macbeth <u>placed</u> the responsibility on his wife
         b   **c**
<u>instead</u>. <u>No error.</u>
    d   **e**

69. <u>Because</u> Phillip has a nasty case of the stomach flu, he <u>hasn't ate</u> a single bite of food in <u>more</u> than three
    a   **b** **c**   **d**
days. <u>No error.</u>
        e

70. Because so many novice <u>writers</u> receive innumerable rejection slips, <u>regardless</u> of <u>their</u> basic abilities,
                           a   **b**   **c**
<u>one often gets</u> terribly discouraged. <u>No error.</u>
    d   **e**

71. Tracy <u>had been waiting</u> for her package from UPS for more than a <u>week</u>; her grandmother <u>was sending</u> her
           a   b   c
several jars of homemade jam <u>and</u> some of her famous chocolate chip cookies. <u>No error.</u>
                          d   e

72. I get along fairly <u>good</u> with my younger sister Jennifer, <u>but</u> when we had to <u>share</u> the same room, we <u>fought</u>
                   a   b   c   d
on an hourly basis the majority of the time. <u>No error.</u>
                             e

73. Mrs. Hammerhill <u>was</u> an amazing piano teacher; she was the only person <u>which</u> <u>taught</u> her students how
                  a   b c
<u>to play</u> with their heart and soul, instead of by memorizing notes and finger positions. <u>No error.</u>
  d   e

74. One of my favorite books of all time <u>being</u> *Replay*, about a man who <u>gets the chance</u> to live his life over and
                                   a   b
over again, each time <u>remembering</u> his former lives and choosing a different path <u>to follow</u>. <u>No error.</u>
                  c   d   e

75. <u>Reading through the local daily newspaper,</u> <u>it</u> always features the current news, regular comic strips, classified
                       a   b
ads, movie <u>listings</u>, and, <u>of course</u>, current sports' scores. <u>No error.</u>
             c   d   e

76. The physicians <u>particularly</u> enjoyed the afternoon workshop offered by the retired doctor <u>who</u> <u>has been</u> to
                 a   b   c
India <u>during</u> a serious outbreak of smallpox. <u>No error.</u>
        d   e

77. The hours went by <u>so slow</u> while she sat in the dentist's chair that she could <u>hardly</u> believe <u>it</u> was still
                  a   b   c
daylight when she finally got back out to her car in the <u>parking lot</u>. <u>No error.</u>
                                      d   e

78. The post office, public libraries, and schools <u>were all closed</u> for the <u>holiday, however</u>, the bank <u>was</u> still
                                           a   b   c
open, much to <u>my</u> relief. <u>No error.</u>
             d   e

79. The teenager <u>repeatedly stated</u> how pleased <u>he was</u> that the temporary argument between <u>we</u> and them had
                a   **b**   **c**

been settled so <u>quickly</u> and easily. <u>No error.</u>
            d   **e**

80. <u>My mother</u> is <u>preparing</u> for the big family party by ordering the flowers, putting up the decorations,
     a   **b**

cooking the food, and <u>to bake</u> enough cookies to send a dozen home with <u>each person</u>. <u>No error.</u>
                c   **d**   **e**

81. The <u>historic old house</u> was due <u>to be torn down</u> that <u>weekend;</u> I was adamant that we could stop it from
         a   **b**   **c**

happening if we just gathered enough people <u>to protest</u> the destruction of a piece of local history. <u>No error.</u>
                                   d   **e**

82. Neither of the shampoo commercials <u>were</u> <u>remotely</u> interesting to me, so I <u>was</u> more grateful than ever for
                                 a   **b**   **c**

the mute button on <u>my</u> television remote. <u>No error.</u>
                 d   **e**

83. Had she only <u>done like</u> I had told her, what <u>should have been</u> a tight, logical, and smooth <u>debate</u> against the
                  a   **b**   **c**

rival high school team would not have turned into such a devastating and monumental loss for <u>our team</u>.
                                                                               d

<u>No error.</u>
  e

84. The telephone rang <u>repeated</u>, and within <u>less than</u> an hour, the answering machine was completely full of
                            a   **b**

messages from people <u>who</u> <u>were</u> concerned about me. <u>No error.</u>
                     c   **d**   **e**

85. <u>Considering</u> how exhausted she was, I think that <u>my</u> grandmother should not <u>have attempted</u> to clean the
      a   **b**   **c**

house as <u>thorough</u> as she did. <u>No error.</u>
          d   **e**

86. <u>To teach</u> a class <u>well</u>, you need <u>to know</u> the material thoroughly, pay close attention to the students, show a
     a   **b**   **c**

sincere interest in the topic, and <u>be willing</u> to go back over the more complicated details. <u>No error.</u>
                              d   **e**

87. In the latest murder mystery by <u>my</u> all-time favorite author, he <u>made sure</u> <u>to include</u> an evil villain, some
                                  a   **b**   **c**

     <u>confusing</u> clues, a bumbling detective, and a twist-filled ending. <u>No error.</u>
     d   **e**

88. While a person's health may be affected by a number of factors, it is illogical for <u>one</u> to think that <u>daily</u>
                                                                               a   **b**

     nutrition, exercise, stress, and sleep will not gradually <u>over some time</u> <u>make</u> a significant difference.
                                                                c   **d**

     <u>No error.</u>
     e

89. <u>While</u> the number of coffee shops opening in cities like Portland and Seattle <u>keep</u> expanding, business
     a   **b**

     owners <u>continue</u> to invest in this <u>highly</u> competitive market. <u>No error.</u>
             c   **d**   **e**

90. <u>Despite</u> continued warning labels and aggressive advertising campaigns on radio and television, there <u>is</u>
     a   **b**

     still an <u>astonishing</u> number of young adults <u>who</u> are smoking cigarettes on a daily basis. <u>No error.</u>
                    c   **d**   **e**

91. High above the Pacific Ocean <u>rises</u> the <u>brilliantly</u> painted clouds <u>reflecting</u> the sun's very <u>last remnants</u> of
                                a   **b**   **c**   **d**

     light. <u>No error.</u>
            e

92. <u>Poor writing</u>, along with inadequate <u>research skills</u> and out-of-date information, <u>are</u> among the main
     a   **b**   **c**

     reasons a term paper will get a <u>failing</u> grade in this class. <u>No error.</u>
                                   d   **e**

93. Several witnesses <u>seen</u> the defendant <u>running away</u> from the scene of the crime, <u>according to</u> court records
                          a   **b**   **c**

     of <u>their</u> testimony. <u>No error.</u>
        d   **e**

94. <u>According</u> to the daily newspaper and television headlines, <u>there is</u> a <u>multitude of reasons</u> that gasoline
     a   **b**   **c**

     prices continue <u>to climb</u> with every passing week. <u>No error.</u>
                    d   **e**

95. The <u>imminent</u> professor <u>was delighted</u> to see that the college auditorium was <u>completely</u> filled with
          a   **b**   **c**

students eager to hear <u>his</u> lecture on the recent controversy over stem cell research. <u>No error.</u>
                d   **e**

96. Once my sister Katherine knew I <u>was ready</u>, she <u>thrown</u> the ball at me so I could practice <u>catching it</u> with
                               a   **b**   **c**

the brand-new baseball mitt I <u>had gotten</u> for my birthday. <u>No error.</u>
                          d   **e**

97. Often <u>mistaken for</u> termites, carpenter ants have longer bodies and <u>shorter wings than</u> termites, <u>and while</u>
             a   **b**   **c**

termite antennae are straight, the antennae of the carpenter variety <u>is</u> bent or "elbowed." <u>No error.</u>
                                               d   **e**

98. The classified ad in today's newspaper <u>suggested</u> that <u>only</u> persons <u>with a Volkswagen bus</u> built between
                                   a   **b**   **c**

1960 and 1970 <u>attend</u> the repair workshop. <u>No error.</u>
              d   **e**

99. <u>Him</u> and the other guys on the high school track team went to the coach's house after <u>the meet</u> <u>for</u> a
       a   **b**   **c**

victory celebration <u>complete with</u> unlimited amounts of pizza and soda. <u>No error.</u>
                        d   **e**

100. <u>Surprisingly</u> enough, in the long line in front of the new coffee shop, <u>barely no one</u> <u>had ever heard</u> of the
        a   **b**   **c**

group that was going to be <u>appearing</u> that afternoon. <u>No error.</u>
                        d   **e**

101. As much as I have tried to <u>adopt</u> to <u>living out</u> in the country, I just <u>can not get used to</u> the silence at
                                a   **b**   **c**

night, the roosters crowing <u>in the morning,</u> or the lack of neighbors for miles around me. <u>No error.</u>
                                d   **e**

102. <u>Despite</u> the company's focus <u>on cultural diversity</u>, the office manager <u>apparently</u> <u>discriminated to</u> hiring
        a   **b**   **c**   **d**

female applicants. <u>No error.</u>
               e

103. For as long as I have known Tamra, she <u>has been</u> <u>inflicted</u> with severe <u>daily</u> headaches that simply do not
　　　　　　　　　　　　　　　　　　　a　　　　　b　　　　　　　　c

<u>respond</u> to any kind of traditional or alternative medicine. <u>No error.</u>
　d　　　　　　　　　　　　　　　　　　　　　　　　　　　　e

104. <u>By the end</u> of the school year, Julia could not believe <u>it</u> when her coach <u>told her</u> that she <u>had swum</u> more
　a　　　　　　　　　　　　　　　　　　　　　　　　b　　　　　　　　c　　　　　　　d

than 20 miles just in practice laps. <u>No error.</u>
　　　　　　　　　　　　　　　　　e

105. Although musicals <u>are</u> <u>apparently</u> no longer popular, <u>but</u> I will continue <u>to watch</u> my old favorites,
　　　　　　　　　　a　　　b　　　　　　　　　　　　c　　　　　　　　　d

including *The Unsinkable Molly Brown*, *Seven Brides for Seven Brothers*, and *My Fair Lady*. <u>No error.</u>
　　　e

106. A number of <u>musical artists</u> produce an average of <u>one album per year</u>, but due to the <u>constant play time</u>
　　　　　　　　a　　　　　　　　　　　　　　　b　　　　　　　　　　　　　　c

of individual songs on the radio, <u>appeared</u> to release quite a bit more. <u>No error.</u>
　　　　　　　　　　　　　　d　　　　　　　　　　　　　　　　e

107. <u>You</u> can never truly save enough money <u>because</u> you never know when <u>anything</u> from a horrible
　a　　　　　　　　　　　　　　　　　b　　　　　　　　　　　　　c

catastrophe to an <u>unbelievable opportunity</u> might knock at your door. <u>No error.</u>
　　　　　　　　　d　　　　　　　　　　　　　　　　　　　　e

108. <u>According</u> to recent surveys, families who take the time to <u>regular</u> <u>eat</u> meals together demonstrate closer
　a　　　　　　　　　　　　　　　　　　　　　　b　　c

relationships, <u>increased</u> levels of communication, and a strong sense of unity. <u>No error.</u>
　　　　　d　　　　　　　　　　　　　　　　　　　　　　　　e

109. A veteran carpenter <u>traditionally</u> keeps <u>their</u> various tools in excellent condition by <u>storing them</u> in a
　　　　　　　　　　a　　　　　b　　　　　　　　　　　　　　　　c

dry, safe place and replacing anything that cannot be <u>easily</u> repaired. <u>No error.</u>
　　　　　　　　　　　　　　　　　　　　d　　　　　　　　e

110. <u>Despite</u> the dire forest fire warnings for the surrounding area, there <u>are</u> still hundreds of stubborn
　a　　　　　　　　　　　　　　　　　　　　　　　　　　b

homeowners <u>who</u> refuse to take any of the <u>necessary precautions</u>. <u>No error.</u>
　　　　　c　　　　　　　　　　d　　　　　e

111. Through the front gates of the Graceland mansion <u>passes</u> thousands of visitors <u>who</u> have come <u>to pay</u>
                                                 a   **b**   **c**

<u>their</u> respects to Elvis, the King of Rock and Roll. <u>No error.</u>
  d   **e**

112. My favorite clowns <u>are</u> the ones <u>which</u> look like they are going to throw a bucket of water out into the
                                a   **b**

audience, but at the last minute, they pour <u>it</u> on their heads and it is <u>actually</u> just torn up pieces of paper.
                                               c   **d**

<u>No error.</u>
  e

113. Half <u>of the students</u> in the class stayed up all night in order to <u>work in</u> the questions that <u>confused</u> them
             a   **b**   **c**

the <u>most</u>. <u>No error.</u>
    d   **e**

114. Identifying sentence errors, <u>although</u> <u>helpful</u> for preparing for the SAT, can be quite <u>tedious</u> once <u>you</u> have
                               a   **b**   **c**   **d**

read more than a hundred of them. <u>No error.</u>
                                     e

▶ Answers

1. b. This statement uses a double negative. Both *isn't* and *hardly* are both negatives. The *isn't* should be changed to *is*.

2. b. When two things are compared, an adjective in the comparative degree is needed. The *best* should be *better*.

3. c. This question contains an error in pronoun shift. The sentence begins with *you* but changes at the end to *one*. You have to be consistent all the way through from beginning to end.

4. c. The subject of the sentence is *gathering*, which is singular. The verb should also be singular, so the *were* should be *was*.

5. e. There is no error in this example.

6. b. There is an error in diction in this sentence. An adverb is needed to modify the verb *rang*. *Unexpected* should be *unexpectedly*.

7. b. This question tests an error in diction. Adverbs modify active verbs, and it should be *well* instead of *good* to modify the verb *to write*.

8. d. This sentence contains faulty parallelism. Coordinating elements in a series should have parallel grammatical form. *Swimming in the chilly ocean* should be *swim in the chilly ocean*.

9. b. The problem here is the pronoun shift. The sentence starts in the third person, using *one*. To be consistent, the next pronoun used should be *one*, not *you*.

10. b. This sentence demonstrates a problem with subject-verb agreement. The subject is *writers*, which is plural. This requires a plural verb, so *appears* should be *appear*.

11. c. You should not use *however* as a conjunction between independent clauses. There should be either a semicolon or a period.

12. c. This is an example of a problem with pronoun/ antecedent agreement. The antecedents are *guests* and *members*, which are plural, so the pronoun should be plural also. *His or her* should be *their*.

13. c. Here is a problem with pronoun reference. The pronoun *they* does not refer to any specific noun or pronoun.

14. a. The subject is *neither*, which is singular. The verb needs to be singular, too, so the *are* should be *is*.

15. a. This is a question about faulty comparison. A comparison of two things uses the comparative degree by adding *-er*. The word *scariest* should be *scarier*.

16. c. This is a run-on sentence. You cannot join two independent clauses with a comma. It needs to be replaced with either a period or semicolon.

17. e. There is no error in this question.

18. d. It is incorrect to use a pronoun in the wrong number. The subject is singular (*student*), and the pronoun should also be singular. The word *their* should be *his or her*.

19. d. Here is a problem with faulty parallelism. The verbs in the sentence all end in *-ing* (*including, paying, stopping*) and *to make out* does not fit this pattern. It should be *making out*.

20. d. You should only use *I* when it is the subject pronoun (it is performing some kind of action). In this case, *I* is the object of a preposition (*between*), so *you and I* should be replaced with *you and me*.

21. b. The issue here is pronoun agreement. The subject is *fire department*, and it is singular, so the pronoun needs to be singular, too. The pronoun *they* should be *it*.

22. c. This is a problem with subject-verb agreement. The subject is *team*, which is singular. The verb should be singular, too. The verb *were* should be *was*.

23. e. There is no error in this question.

24. d. You need to spot an error in verb tense. If you look at the other verbs in the sentence (*revealed, asked, responded*), they are all in the past tense. The phrase *are quiet* should be *were quiet* in order to be consistent.

25. e. When you have a fraction in a sentence, the object of the preposition determines the number of the verb. In this case, the object is *planet*, which is singular, so the verb *was* is correct.

26. c. As with fractions, when you use percentages, the number of the verb is determined by the object of the preposition. Because *class* is singular, the verb needs to be singular, too. The verb *are* should be *is*.

27. c. This is an error with subject-verb agreement. The subject of the sentence is *neither* (not *candidates*). Because it is singular, the verb needs to be singular, too. The verb *have* should be *has*.

28. c. This is an error with subject-verb agreement. Don't be misled by intervening phrases like *as well as his famous poems like 'The Jabber-wocky.'* The subject is *bulk*, which is singular, and the verb should be *is*, not *are*.

29. b. When the subject of the sentence (*stage*) follows the verb, the verb still takes its number from the subject. Because *stage* is singular, the verb needs to be singular, too. *Were* should be *was*.

30. e. There is no error in this question.

31. d. Like the words ending in *-body*, the ones ending in *-one* may sound plural, but they are singular. In this case, the subject is *anyone*, and the verb should be *is* instead of *are*.

32. b. This sentence uses a double negative. *Isn't* and *hardly* are both negatives. *Isn't* should be changed to *is*.

33. c. This question tests subject-verb agreement. Compound nouns require a plural verb. *Guarantees* should be *guarantee*.

34. e. There are no errors in this sentence.

35. d. There is a problem with the pronoun shift in this sentence. The sentence shifts from using *you* to using *one's*. To be consistent, *one's* should be changed to *your*.

36. d. This is a diction error. An adverb is needed to modify the verb. *Quick* should be *quickly*.

37. c. Here, you need to spot a problem with pronoun reference. The pronoun *they* does not refer to any specific noun.

38. d. This is an example of faulty parallelism. Verbs that are in a series should be in parallel form (*cutting, sweeping*), so *pick up* should be *picking up*.

39. a. This statement contains a diction error. Adverbs modify active verbs. You need to use *well* instead of *good* to modify *to mow*.

40. c. The phrase *my sister and I* is the object of the preposition *between*. Use the objective-case pronoun *me* instead.

41. a. *Swear* is an irregular verb, and the past tense should be *swore*, not *sweared*.

42. b. This sentence contains a double negative. The word *no* should be *any*.

43. b. This is a question about subject-verb agreement. *Attitude* is singular, and the verb needs to be singular, too. The verb *were* should be replaced with *was*.

44. a. This is a case of faulty comparison. The word *longest* should be *longer*.

45. e. There are no errors in this sentence.

46. c. The subject *diversity and excitement* is plural, but the verb (*defines*) is singular. It should be replaced with *define*.

47. c. A possessive pronoun is needed before a gerund. *Him* should be replaced with *his*.

48. b. The noun *people* is singular, and the verb needs to be singular, too. In this case, you need to change *does* to *do*.

49. d. This question deals with pronoun reference. The pronoun *it* does not refer to any specific noun or pronoun.

50. a. This question looks at the comparative degree. A comparison of two things requires an adjective in the comparative degree. Use *better* instead of *the best*.

51. b. You must spot a mistake in verb tense. *Fight* is an irregular verb, so *fighted* should be changed to *fought*.

52. a. Standard usage requires the use of *who* rather than *which* when referring to people (*teachers*).

53. c. This sentence contains a pronoun shift. The sentence started out with *you* and then shifted to *one*. *One* should be replaced by *you* for consistency.

54. a. Standard usage requires the use of *who* rather than *which* when referring to people (*skaters*).

55. b. This is a case of an indefinite pronoun. The word *they* does not clearly refer to any noun.

56. c. Here is an idiom error. Standard usage dictates that you use *different from* rather than *different than*.

57. b. This is a case of faulty comparison. The word *other* should be included in a comparison of one thing with a group of which it is a member. The phrase *any other* should read *any other book*.

58. c. This sentence shows a pronoun shift. It starts out as *one* and switches to *you*. To be consistent, *you* should be replaced with *one*.

59. b. The sentence includes an indefinite pronoun. *They* does not relate to any other noun or pronoun.

60. c. You need to identify the verb tense problems. Because *shake* is an irregular verb, the past tense is not formed by adding *-ed*. *Shaked* should be replaced with *shook*.

61. b. This is a question about comparative degree. A comparison of two things requires an adjective in the comparative degree. You should use *better* instead of *the best*.

62. e. There are no errors in this sentence.

63. b. This sentence contains a double negative. Both *isn't* and *hardly* are negative. Change *isn't* to *is* to repair the problem.

64. b. The sentence begins with *he* and then switches to *I*. To fix the pronoun shift, *I* should be replaced with *he*.

65. e. There are no errors in this question.

66. b. The sentence begins with a dependent clause, so it must be followed by an independent clause. Taking out the word *but* will repair the problem and make it correct.

67. d. This question has a problem with pronoun/antecedent agreement. The pronoun *their* is plural; the antecedent is *disc jockey*, which is singular. Instead, use the pronoun *his* or *her*.

68. c. This sentence has a problem with verb tense. The sentence is cast in the present tense, so *placed* should be *places*.

69. c. Because *eat* is an irregular verb, the past tense does not get an *-ed*. The word *ate* should be changed to *eaten*, because of the helping verb (*has*).

70. d. In this sentence, the pronoun shifts. The sentence begins with *writers* and correctly uses the pronoun *their*, but then switches to the pronoun *one*. *One often gets* should be replaced with *they often get*.

71. e. There are no errors in this sentence.

72. a. An adverb is needed to modify *get*. Use *well* (an adverb) instead of *good* (an adjective).

73. b. Use *which* for things and *who* for people.

74. a. This is a sentence fragment; it lacks a main verb. The *-ing* form of *to be* (*being*) cannot be used as the main verb; use *is* instead.

75. a. This is an example of a dangling participle. This sentence, as written, indicates that the newspaper (*it*) was reading: The subject of the main clause of a sentence is assumed to be the subject of the phrase attached to the main clause. It is not logical for the newspaper to read through the local daily newspaper. The phrase *reading through the local daily newspaper* lacks the correct noun or pronoun to modify.

76. c. This sentence has a problem with verb tense. The past perfect tense is used to refer to action completed prior to a specific time in the past. You should replace *has been* with *had been*.

77. a. An adverb is needed to modify the verb *went*. *Slow* should be replaced with *slowly*.

78. b. Do not use *however* as a conjunction between independent clauses. Use a semicolon or a period instead.

79. c. This example has a problem with the pronoun case. The object of the preposition *between* should be in the objective case. Use *us* instead of *we*.

80. c. You need to identify the faulty parallelism. Coordinate items in a series should be in the same grammatical form, so *to bake* should be *baking*.

81. e. There are no errors in this example.

82. a. Here is a problem with subject-verb agreement. *Neither* is singular, so *were* should be *was* for consistency.

83. a. This is a tricky diction error. *Like* is a preposition and should not be used in place of a conjunction. Replace *like* with *as*.

84. a. The word *repeated* modifies *rang*, so it needs to be in adverb form. It should be replaced with *repeatedly*.

85. d. An adverb is needed to modify the verb *clean*, so *thorough* should be replaced with *thoroughly*.

86. e. There are no errors in this sentence.

87. e. There are no errors in this sentence.

88. c. Here is an example of wordiness. The phrase *over some time* is identical in meaning to *gradually*, so you can eliminate it to avoid redundancy.

89. b. In this sentence, it may seem like the subject is *shops*, but it is actually *number*, which is a singular noun. The verb *keep* needs to be singular, too, so it should be changed to *keeps*.

90. b. This is an example of subject-verb agreement when the subject follows the verb. The subject in this sentence is *adults*, which is plural. The verb *is* should be replaced with *are*, so that it is plural, too.

91. a. Although it may seem like the subject is *Pacific Ocean*, the subject is actually *clouds*, which is plural. The verb *rises* needs to be plural, too, so it should be changed to *rise*.

92. c. The subject of this sentence is *poor writing*. The verb *are* should be singular to match the subject, so change *are* to *is*.

93. a. Here, you can identify confusion between the simple past and the past participle. *Seen* should only be used with a helping verb. The word should be replaced with *saw*, which is the simple past tense of the verb.

94. b. The subject here is *reasons*, which is plural. The verb should be *are*, not *is*.

95. a. This is a simple case of the wrong word choice. *Imminent* means something that is likely to happen soon. The correct word for this sentence is *eminent*, which means out-standing or prominent.

96. b. This sentence confuses the simple past and the past participle. *Thrown* should only be used with a helping verb. It should be replaced with *threw*, which is the simple past tense of the verb.

97. d. The subject of the verb *is* is *antennae*, a plural noun. Thus, the verb must be the plural *are*. The prepositional phrase *of the carpenter variety* may mislead you to believe that *variety* is the subject, but subjects are never in a prepositional phrase.

98. c. Here is a problem with number agreement. Nouns in a sentence must have logical number relationships. The noun here is *persons*, which is plural. However, the second noun is *bus*. It should also be plural. The underlined phrase should read *with Volkswagen buses.*

99. a. The compound subject in this sentence is *him and the guys on high school track team.* The pronoun *him* is in the object form of the pronoun in the third-person singular; it is wrong because the pronoun is the subject. *Him* should be replaced with *he*.

100. b. To correct the double negative, replace *barely no one* with *barely anyone* or *hardly anyone*.

101. a. This is an example of incorrect word choice. The word *adopt* means to make something one's own. In this sentence, the correct word should be *adapt*, which means to change something or make it suitable for a specific use or purpose.

102. d. This is a case of using the wrong preposition. Standard usage dictates using *discriminated against*, not *discriminated to*.

103. b. You need to identify the incorrect word choice. The word *inflicted* means to impose punishment or suffering on someone. The correct word to use is *afflicted*, which means the causing of pain, suffering, or annoyance on someone.

104. e. There are no errors in this sentence.

105. c. This is an example of a dependent clause being followed by another dependent clause, which is not grammatically correct. To repair the sentence, remove *but*.

106. d. This has an error in verb tense. The sentence starts out in the present tense (*produce*) but then changes to the past tense (*appeared*). To repair the error, change *appeared* to *appear*.

107. e. There are no errors in this sentence.

108. b. The word *regular* is modifying the verb *eat*, so it needs to be in adverb form. Change *regular* to *regularly*.

109. b. You need to identify an error in pronoun agreement. The subject is *carpenter*, which is singular. The possessive pronoun should be *his* or *her*, not the plural *their*.

110. e. There are no errors in this sentence.

111. a. The subject in this sentence is *thousands of visitors*, which is plural, not *mansion*. The verb has to be plural, so *passes* should be *pass*.

112. b. Clowns are people, not things. Use *who* instead of *which*.

113. b. This sentence contains an incorrect preposition. According to standard usage, the term *work in* should be *work out* or *figure out*.

114. e. There are no errors in this sentence.

CHAPTER

3 ▶ Improving Sentences Questions

The following are examples of the different improving sentences questions you may be tested on in the SAT. There are 161 questions here to practice, so by the time you get to the last one, you will be well prepared to tackle this section of the SAT!

IMPROVING SENTENCES

1.	(a)	(b)	(c)	(d)	(e)	51.	(a)	(b)	(c)	(d)	(e)	101.	(a)	(b)	(c)	(d)	(e)
2.	(a)	(b)	(c)	(d)	(e)	52.	(a)	(b)	(c)	(d)	(e)	102.	(a)	(b)	(c)	(d)	(e)
3.	(a)	(b)	(c)	(d)	(e)	53.	(a)	(b)	(c)	(d)	(e)	103.	(a)	(b)	(c)	(d)	(e)
4.	(a)	(b)	(c)	(d)	(e)	54.	(a)	(b)	(c)	(d)	(e)	104.	(a)	(b)	(c)	(d)	(e)
5.	(a)	(b)	(c)	(d)	(e)	55.	(a)	(b)	(c)	(d)	(e)	105.	(a)	(b)	(c)	(d)	(e)
6.	(a)	(b)	(c)	(d)	(e)	56.	(a)	(b)	(c)	(d)	(e)	106.	(a)	(b)	(c)	(d)	(e)
7.	(a)	(b)	(c)	(d)	(e)	57.	(a)	(b)	(c)	(d)	(e)	107.	(a)	(b)	(c)	(d)	(e)
8.	(a)	(b)	(c)	(d)	(e)	58.	(a)	(b)	(c)	(d)	(e)	108.	(a)	(b)	(c)	(d)	(e)
9.	(a)	(b)	(c)	(d)	(e)	59.	(a)	(b)	(c)	(d)	(e)	109.	(a)	(b)	(c)	(d)	(e)
10.	(a)	(b)	(c)	(d)	(e)	60.	(a)	(b)	(c)	(d)	(e)	110.	(a)	(b)	(c)	(d)	(e)
11.	(a)	(b)	(c)	(d)	(e)	61.	(a)	(b)	(c)	(d)	(e)	111.	(a)	(b)	(c)	(d)	(e)
12.	(a)	(b)	(c)	(d)	(e)	62.	(a)	(b)	(c)	(d)	(e)	112.	(a)	(b)	(c)	(d)	(e)
13.	(a)	(b)	(c)	(d)	(e)	63.	(a)	(b)	(c)	(d)	(e)	113.	(a)	(b)	(c)	(d)	(e)
14.	(a)	(b)	(c)	(d)	(e)	64.	(a)	(b)	(c)	(d)	(e)	114.	(a)	(b)	(c)	(d)	(e)
15.	(a)	(b)	(c)	(d)	(e)	65.	(a)	(b)	(c)	(d)	(e)	115.	(a)	(b)	(c)	(d)	(e)
16.	(a)	(b)	(c)	(d)	(e)	66.	(a)	(b)	(c)	(d)	(e)	116.	(a)	(b)	(c)	(d)	(e)
17.	(a)	(b)	(c)	(d)	(e)	67.	(a)	(b)	(c)	(d)	(e)	117.	(a)	(b)	(c)	(d)	(e)
18.	(a)	(b)	(c)	(d)	(e)	68.	(a)	(b)	(c)	(d)	(e)	118.	(a)	(b)	(c)	(d)	(e)
19.	(a)	(b)	(c)	(d)	(e)	69.	(a)	(b)	(c)	(d)	(e)	119.	(a)	(b)	(c)	(d)	(e)
20.	(a)	(b)	(c)	(d)	(e)	70.	(a)	(b)	(c)	(d)	(e)	120.	(a)	(b)	(c)	(d)	(e)
21.	(a)	(b)	(c)	(d)	(e)	71.	(a)	(b)	(c)	(d)	(e)	121.	(a)	(b)	(c)	(d)	(e)
22.	(a)	(b)	(c)	(d)	(e)	72.	(a)	(b)	(c)	(d)	(e)	122.	(a)	(b)	(c)	(d)	(e)
23.	(a)	(b)	(c)	(d)	(e)	73.	(a)	(b)	(c)	(d)	(e)	123.	(a)	(b)	(c)	(d)	(e)
24.	(a)	(b)	(c)	(d)	(e)	74.	(a)	(b)	(c)	(d)	(e)	124.	(a)	(b)	(c)	(d)	(e)
25.	(a)	(b)	(c)	(d)	(e)	75.	(a)	(b)	(c)	(d)	(e)	125.	(a)	(b)	(c)	(d)	(e)
26.	(a)	(b)	(c)	(d)	(e)	76.	(a)	(b)	(c)	(d)	(e)	126.	(a)	(b)	(c)	(d)	(e)
27.	(a)	(b)	(c)	(d)	(e)	77.	(a)	(b)	(c)	(d)	(e)	127.	(a)	(b)	(c)	(d)	(e)
28.	(a)	(b)	(c)	(d)	(e)	78.	(a)	(b)	(c)	(d)	(e)	128.	(a)	(b)	(c)	(d)	(e)
29.	(a)	(b)	(c)	(d)	(e)	79.	(a)	(b)	(c)	(d)	(e)	129.	(a)	(b)	(c)	(d)	(e)
30.	(a)	(b)	(c)	(d)	(e)	80.	(a)	(b)	(c)	(d)	(e)	130.	(a)	(b)	(c)	(d)	(e)
31.	(a)	(b)	(c)	(d)	(e)	81.	(a)	(b)	(c)	(d)	(e)	131.	(a)	(b)	(c)	(d)	(e)
32.	(a)	(b)	(c)	(d)	(e)	82.	(a)	(b)	(c)	(d)	(e)	132.	(a)	(b)	(c)	(d)	(e)
33.	(a)	(b)	(c)	(d)	(e)	83.	(a)	(b)	(c)	(d)	(e)	133.	(a)	(b)	(c)	(d)	(e)
34.	(a)	(b)	(c)	(d)	(e)	84.	(a)	(b)	(c)	(d)	(e)	134.	(a)	(b)	(c)	(d)	(e)
35.	(a)	(b)	(c)	(d)	(e)	85.	(a)	(b)	(c)	(d)	(e)	135.	(a)	(b)	(c)	(d)	(e)
36.	(a)	(b)	(c)	(d)	(e)	86.	(a)	(b)	(c)	(d)	(e)	136.	(a)	(b)	(c)	(d)	(e)
37.	(a)	(b)	(c)	(d)	(e)	87.	(a)	(b)	(c)	(d)	(e)	137.	(a)	(b)	(c)	(d)	(e)
38.	(a)	(b)	(c)	(d)	(e)	88.	(a)	(b)	(c)	(d)	(e)	138.	(a)	(b)	(c)	(d)	(e)
39.	(a)	(b)	(c)	(d)	(e)	89.	(a)	(b)	(c)	(d)	(e)	139.	(a)	(b)	(c)	(d)	(e)
40.	(a)	(b)	(c)	(d)	(e)	90.	(a)	(b)	(c)	(d)	(e)	140.	(a)	(b)	(c)	(d)	(e)
41.	(a)	(b)	(c)	(d)	(e)	91.	(a)	(b)	(c)	(d)	(e)	141.	(a)	(b)	(c)	(d)	(e)
42.	(a)	(b)	(c)	(d)	(e)	92.	(a)	(b)	(c)	(d)	(e)	142.	(a)	(b)	(c)	(d)	(e)
43.	(a)	(b)	(c)	(d)	(e)	93.	(a)	(b)	(c)	(d)	(e)	143.	(a)	(b)	(c)	(d)	(e)
44.	(a)	(b)	(c)	(d)	(e)	94.	(a)	(b)	(c)	(d)	(e)	144.	(a)	(b)	(c)	(d)	(e)
45.	(a)	(b)	(c)	(d)	(e)	95.	(a)	(b)	(c)	(d)	(e)	145.	(a)	(b)	(c)	(d)	(e)
46.	(a)	(b)	(c)	(d)	(e)	96.	(a)	(b)	(c)	(d)	(e)	146.	(a)	(b)	(c)	(d)	(e)
47.	(a)	(b)	(c)	(d)	(e)	97.	(a)	(b)	(c)	(d)	(e)	147.	(a)	(b)	(c)	(d)	(e)
48.	(a)	(b)	(c)	(d)	(e)	98.	(a)	(b)	(c)	(d)	(e)	148.	(a)	(b)	(c)	(d)	(e)
49.	(a)	(b)	(c)	(d)	(e)	99.	(a)	(b)	(c)	(d)	(e)	149.	(a)	(b)	(c)	(d)	(e)
50.	(a)	(b)	(c)	(d)	(e)	100.	(a)	(b)	(c)	(d)	(e)	150.	(a)	(b)	(c)	(d)	(e)

151. (a) (b) (c) (d) (e)
152. (a) (b) (c) (d) (e)
153. (a) (b) (c) (d) (e)
154. (a) (b) (c) (d) (e)
155. (a) (b) (c) (d) (e)
156. (a) (b) (c) (d) (e)

157. (a) (b) (c) (d) (e)
158. (a) (b) (c) (d) (e)
159. (a) (b) (c) (d) (e)
160. (a) (b) (c) (d) (e)
161. (a) (b) (c) (d) (e)

▶ Questions

1. Although meteorologists continue to get more and more advanced technology and equipment, <u>their weather forecasts wrong</u> about 50% of the time.
   a. their weather forecasts wrong
   b. their weather forecasts which is wrong
   c. their weather forecasts are wrong
   d. is their weather forecasts wrong
   e. their weather forecasts that is wrong

2. Some couples have their first child before they have learned any real parenting skills, <u>while a few reading books and attending seminars as soon as they find out they are pregnant.</u>
   a. while a few reading books and attending seminars as soon as they find out they are pregnant.
   b. while a few, reading books and attending seminars as soon as they find out they are pregnant.
   c. but a few reading books and attending seminars as soon as they find out they are pregnant.
   d. however, a few reading books and attending seminars as soon as they find out they are pregnant.
   e. while a few begin reading books and attending seminars as soon as they find out they are pregnant.

3. The number of grocery store shoppers that carry a wallet full of coupons with them <u>is growing, approximately 50%</u> of those in line have at least one applicable coupon to apply to their purchases.
   a. is growing, approximately 50%
   b. is growing; approximately 50%
   c. is growing, although approximately 50%
   d. is grown, approximately 50%
   e. is to grown, approximately 50%

4. <u>Raymond's new vacuum worked beautifully</u> on the interior of his new car, he still was not able to get the pine needles from last year's Christmas tree out of the side pockets.
   a. Raymond's new vacuum worked beautifully
   b. Because Raymond's new vacuum worked beautifully
   c. Although Raymond's new vacuum worked beautifully
   d. Raymond's new vacuum worked beautifully,
   e. Whenever Raymond's new vacuum worked beautifully

5. <u>After watching television for more than seven hours straight, the couch no longer felt very comfortable to the young boys.</u>
   a. After watching television for more than seven hours straight, the couch no longer felt very comfortable to the young boys.
   b. After watching television for more than seven hours straight, the young boys were no longer very comfortable on the couch.
   c. Watching television for more than seven hours straight, the couch no longer felt very comfortable to the young boys.
   d. The young boys were no longer very comfortable on the couch, after they had watched television for more than seven hours straight.
   e. For more than seven hours straight the boys had watched television, the couch no longer felt very comfortable to them.

6. To keep her house completely clean, she spends at least three hours a day dusting the furniture, vacuuming the floors, and <u>she puts away a minimum of two loads of laundry.</u>

   a. she puts away a minimum of two loads of laundry.

   b. next, she puts away a minimum of two loads of laundry.

   c. finally, she putting away a minimum of two loads of laundry

   d. putting away a minimum of two loads of laundry she does.

   e. putting away a minimum of two loads of laundry.

7. The character of Clark Kent has been around for decades, <u>because no one has made him quite as popular as Tom Welling has in *Smallville.*</u>

   a. because no one has made him quite as popular as Tom Welling has in *Smallville.*

   b. although no one has made him quite as popular as Tom Welling has in *Smallville.*

   c. since no one has made him quite as popular as Tom Welling has in *Smallville.*

   d. for no one has made him quite as popular as Tom Welling has in *Smallville.*

   e. whenever no one had made him quite as popular as Tom Welling has in *Smallville.*

8. <u>Because the *Serenity* movie was quite popular in the movie theaters and on home video</u>, there are still no plans to bring back the *Firefly* series, according to former producer Joss Whedon.

   a. Because the *Serenity* movie was quite popular in the movie theaters and on home video

   b. Although the *Serenity* movie was quite popular in the movie theaters and on home video

   c. Since the *Serenity* movie was quite popular in the movie theaters and on home video

   d. However, the *Serenity* movie was quite popular in the movie theaters and on home video

   e. For the *Serenity* movies was quite popular in the movie theaters and on home video

9. The Parkinsons have decided to cancel their Saturday afternoon barbeque by the pool <u>while the weather forecast is calling</u> for massive thunderstorms throughout the entire weekend.

   a. while the weather forecast is calling

   b. so the weather forecast is calling

   c. although the weather forecast is calling

   d. however the weather forecast is calling

   e. since the weather forecast is calling

10. Situation comedies have been popular with audiences of all ages <u>for the last several decades, some of them have become entrenched</u> into our culture in a number of ways.

   a. for the last several decades, some of them have become entrenched

   b. for the last several decades, become entrenching some of them have

   c. some of them, for the last several decades, have become entrenched

   d. for the last several decades; some of them have become entrenched

   e. becoming entrenched, for the last several decades, they have

11. In the United States, a growing number of families that do not have much spare time on their hands <u>and end up in the drive-through lines</u> at convenient fast-food restaurants.
   a. and end up in the drive-through lines
   b. so end up in the drive-through lines
   c. end up in the drive-through lines
   d. ends up in the drive-through lines
   e. ending up in the drive-through lines

12. Countless music groups and individual singers have recorded a version of "Unchained Melody," <u>no one can perform it better than the original Righteous Brothers though</u>.
   a. no one can perform it better than the original Righteous Brothers though
   b. since no one can perform it better than the original Righteous Brothers though
   c. in performing, no one can do it better than the original Righteous Brothers
   d. The Righteous Brothers perform it better because they are the original
   e. but no one can perform it better than the original Righteous Brothers

13. <u>Whenever the telephone rings,</u> everyone in the house knows that it is going to be for Nicole since she has a social life that is busy enough for at least three people.
   a. Whenever the telephone rings,
   b. The telephone, whenever it rings,
   c. Ringing, whenever the telephone does
   d. Because the telephone rings,
   e. The telephone rings

14. <u>Originally designed to help people control their diabetes, the physician informed the fascinated audience that this medication would also assist thousands in losing significant amounts of weight.</u>
   a. Originally designed to help people control their diabetes, the physician informed the fascinated audience that this medication would also assist thousands in losing significant amounts of weight.
   b. Designed to help people control their diabetes originally, the physician informed the fascinated audience that it would also assist thousands in losing significant amounts of weight.
   c. Originally designed to help people control their diabetes, this medication would also assist thousands in losing significant amounts of weight, the physician told the fascinated audience.
   d. The physician told the fascinated audience that although originally designed to help people control their diabetes, significant amounts of weight could be lost as well with this medication.
   e. Losing significant amounts of weight could be done with the medication originally designed to help people control their diabetes, said the physician to his fascinated audience.

15. While numerous horror novels try to persuade readers that psychopaths are hiding around every corner, <u>other authors much more optimistic.</u>
   a. other authors much more optimistic.
   b. other authors are much more optimistic.
   c. other authors is much more optimistic.
   d. other authors which are much more optimistic.
   e. other authors although much more optimistic.

16. Television detectives miraculously have the ability to solve the most complicated crimes in less than <u>an hour, few can do it</u> with as much style and obsessiveness as the main character on *Monk*.
- **a.** an hour, few can do it
- **b.** an hour since few can do it
- **c.** an hour, for few can do it
- **d.** an hour; few can do it
- **e.** an hour, while few can do it

17. <u>The curious student asked the museum curator endless questions from the local high school history class.</u>
- **a.** The curious student asked the museum curator endless questions from the local high school history class.
- **b.** From the local high school history class, the museum curator was asked endless questions by the curious student.
- **c.** The curious student from the local high school history class asked the museum curator endless questions.
- **d.** Endless questions were asked by the curious student from the local high school to the museum curator.
- **e.** The museum curator asked the curious student from the local high school endless questions.

18. The high wind warning <u>had been issued in the evening; people were already tying down</u> their possessions and preparing for the worst.
- **a.** had been issued in the evening; people were already tying down
- **b.** had been issued in the evening, people were already tying down
- **c.** had been issued in the evening, since people were already tying down
- **d.** had been issued in the evening; already tying down
- **e.** had been issued in the evening for people were already tying down

19. <u>After watching *Jaws* for the fifth time, the ocean looked incredibly menacing to tourists Kathleen and Kevin.</u>
- **a.** After watching *Jaws* for the fifth time, the ocean looked incredibly menacing to Kathleen and Kevin.
- **b.** After watching *Jaws* for the fifth time, incredibly menacing the ocean looked to tourists Kathleen and Kevin.
- **c.** Tourists Kathleen and Kevin, after watching *Jaws* for the fifth time, thought the ocean looked incredibly menacing.
- **d.** The ocean looked incredibly menacing to tourists Kathleen and Kevin who had just watched *Jaws* for the fifth time.
- **e.** After watching *Jaws* for the fifth time, tourists Kathleen and Kevin thought that the ocean looked incredibly menacing.

20. Putting up the Venetian blinds was far more complicated than <u>I had anticipated; it seemed like a difficult puzzle</u> with more than a few pieces missing.
   a. I had anticipated; it seemed like a difficult puzzle
   b. I had anticipated, it seemed like a difficult puzzle
   c. I had anticipated it seemed like a difficult puzzle
   d. I had anticipated since it seemed like a difficult puzzle
   e. I had anticipated so it seemed like a difficult puzzle

21. The witness told his lawyer <u>that he couldn't hardly remember a time</u> that he had felt safe both in his home and at work.
   a. that he couldn't hardly remember a time
   b. when he could not remember a time
   c. that a time could hardly be remembered when
   d. that he could hardly remember a time
   e. he couldn't hardly remember a time

22. During the party, the <u>dancers that came</u> out like brightly colored flowers.
   a. dancers that came out
   b. dancers coming
   c. dancers, which are coming
   d. dancers came
   e. dancers, which came

23. The body has a natural <u>sleep cycle it ranges</u> from six to ten hours a night depending on the individual.
   a. sleep cycles it ranges
   b. sleep cycles, it ranges
   c. sleep cycles; it ranges
   d. sleep cycles since it ranges
   e. sleep cycles when it ranges

24. The American people adore high-tech little <u>gadgets, they buy</u> them as fast as they are produced.
   a. gadgets, they buy
   b. gadgets; they buy
   c. gadgets so they buy
   d. gadgets, they bought
   e. gadgets; buying them

25. The fire was <u>burning brightly; which lit up</u> the night with a fierce orange glow.
   a. burning brightly; which lit up
   b. burning brightly and which lit up
   c. burning brightly, because this lit up
   d. burning brightly which lit up
   e. burning brightly, which lit up

26. Renovating a house takes a lot of money, skill and <u>time; depending</u> on its original condition, what year it was built, and what your goals are.
   a. time; depending
   b. time, depending
   c. time depending
   d. time; thus depending
   e. time, it depends

27. Tom Cruise is one of the country's most recognized <u>actors, he is known</u> for his action-adventure movies, his appearances on talk shows, and his much-publicized romances.
  a. actors, he is known
  b. actors since known
  c. actors; he is known
  d. actors in that he is known
  e. actors most known

28. The birthday cake was already done <u>and the party was not due to start for another hour.</u>
  a. and the party was not due to start for another hour.
  b. since the party was not due to start for another hour.
  c. although the party was not due to start for another hour.
  d. so the party was not due to start for another hour.
  e. the party was not due to start for another hour.

29. When purchasing a car, wise consumers keep in mind how much it costs, what gas mileage it gets, and <u>its safety.</u>
  a. its safety.
  b. if it is safe.
  c. the safety of it.
  d. the ability of it to be safe.
  e. how safe it is.

30. Coping with the cold <u>and enough food</u> made being lost in the forest during the winter even more difficult than she had ever imagined.
  a. and enough food
  b. and finding enough food
  c. and found enough food
  d. and just enough food
  e. and find enough food

31. <u>Having thrown her backpack on her bed, Heather felt deeply disappointed about losing the contest.</u>
  a. Having thrown her backpack on her bed, Heather felt deeply disappointed about losing the contest.
  b. Having felt deeply disappointed about losing the contest, Heather threw her backpack on her bed.
  c. Throwing her backpack on the bed, deeply disappointed about losing the contest Heather was.
  d. Heather lost the contest and threw her backpack on her bed, feeling deeply disappointed.
  e. Deeply disappointed about losing the contest, Heather threw her backpack on her bed.

32. <u>The messenger on the blue 21-speed bicycle with the shiny green pants is on his way to deliver the contract.</u>
  a. The messenger on the blue 21-speed bicycle with the shiny green pants is on his way to deliver the contract.
  b. The messenger on his way to deliver the contact is on the blue 21-speed bicycle with the shiny green pants.
  c. The messenger wearing the shiny green pants and riding the blue 21-speed bicycle is on his way to deliver the contract.
  d. On his way to deliver the contract, the messenger with the shiny green pants and blue 21-speed bicycle is.
  e. With the shiny green pants, the messenger on the blue 21-speed bicycle is on his way to deliver the contract.

33. <u>Heading to the concert</u>, the icy roads made the streets dangerous and slick.
  a. Heading to the concert
  b. While heading to the concert
  c. To head to the concert
  d. While we headed to the concert
  e. En route to the concert

34. I had been taking acting lessons for almost a year before the cast director asks me to join the community playhouse.
  a. cast director asks me to join
  b. cast director being asked to join
  c. cast director asked me to join
  d. cast director had asked me to join
  e. cast director asking me to join

35. Anyone who joins the community choir, regardless of how much vocal experience you have had, should plan to attend the orientation meeting on Monday night.
  a. regardless of how much vocal experience you have had,
  b. irregardless of your personal vocal experience,
  c. regardless of how much vocal experience they have had,
  d. irregardless of their vocal experience,
  e. regardless of vocal experience,

36. Some teachers think that the option of homeschooling and other educational alternatives have created problems within the public school systems.
  a. of homeschooling and other educational alternatives have created problems within the public school systems.
  b. of homeschooling and other educational alternatives has created problems within the public school systems.
  c. of homeschooling and other educational alternatives is created problems within the public school systems.
  d. of homeschooling and other educational alternatives creating problems within the public school systems.
  e. of homeschooling and other educational alternatives has creating problems within the public school systems.

37. The sequel to *Rush Hour* was funnier and more exciting than any sequel I've ever seen.
  a. was funnier and more exciting than any sequel I've ever seen.
  b. was the most funniest and most exciting sequel I've ever seen.
  c. was both funnier and more exciting than any other sequel I've ever seen.
  d. was funnier and most exciting than any movie sequel I've ever seen.
  e. was funnier and more exciting than any other sequel I've ever seen.

38. If you want to see a motorcycle battle like no other, you should watch *Mission Impossible 2*.
  a. like no other, you should watch
  b. like no other; you should watch
  c. like no other you should watch
  d. like no other, you are watching
  e. like no other; so if you watch

39. Because he was given a local anesthetic, Josh was conscience throughout the operation.
  a. Josh was conscience throughout the operation.
  b. Josh had a conscience during the operation.
  c. the operation was completed with Josh conscienceness.
  d. the operation was done while Josh held conscienceness.
  e. Josh remained conscious throughout the operation.

40. Everybody that wants to volunteer to help at the bake sale should put his or her name on the list on the bulletin board.
  a. Everybody that wants to volunteer
  b. Everybody who wants to volunteer
  c. Everybody which wants to volunteer
  d. Everybody wants to volunteer
  e. Everybody wanting to volunteer

41. Both of my grandparents who live in Florida are flying into O'Hare airport this afternoon; they are coming to visit us over the holidays.
  a. Both of my grandparents who live in Florida
  b. My grandparents in Florida
  c. My grandparents, both who live in Florida,
  d. My two grandparents, who lives in Florida,
  e. Both of my grandparents, living in Florida

42. No matter how many times their parents asked them, the twins said they didn't do nothing wrong.
  a. the twins said they didn't do nothing wrong
  b. the twins were saying they didn't do nothing wrong
  c. the twins said they were not doing nothing wrong
  d. the twins they did something wrong
  e. the twins said they did not do anything wrong

43. The firemen responded immediately to the blaring alarm, they had jumped into their suits and piled onto the fire truck in a matter of mere seconds.
  a. blaring alarm, they had jumped
  b. blaring alarm they had jumped
  c. blaring alarm; they were jumping
  d. blaring alarm; they had jumped
  e. blaring alarm because they had jumped

44. Ballroom dancing has made a huge comeback with the younger generations, but it is still not as popular as it was during the 1940s and 1950s.
  a. with the younger generations, but it is still not as popular
  b. with the younger generations; but it is still not as popular
  c. with the younger generations and it is still not as popular
  d. with the younger generations since it is still not as popular
  e. with the younger generations because it is still not as popular

45. They decided to go to the basketball game after all, although one should make plans for something like that long beforehand.
  a. although one should make plans
  b. because one should make plans
  c. although they should have made plans
  d. so they should have made plans
  e. when they decided to make plans

46. Jasmine wanted to attend the opening night of the new Broadway play, but she decides to go to the cocktail party instead.
  a. new Broadway play, but she decides to go
  b. new Broadway play; but she decides to go
  c. new Broadway play, but she decided to go
  d. new Broadway play but she decides to go
  e. new Broadway play but she is deciding to go

47. Everyone who attended the fascinating lecture by the professor <u>knew that their history grade</u> would improve just from listening to what he had to say.
   a. knew that their history grade
   b. knew that his or her history grade
   c. knew that one's history grade
   d. knew that my history grade
   e. knew that our history grade

48. After Louise finished baking ten dozen cookies for her daughter's second-grade class, <u>a trip to the store was made</u> to get plastic bags to hold the treats.
   a. a trip to the store was made
   b. a trip was made to the store
   c. a trip to the store was made by her
   d. she to the store made a trip
   e. she made a trip to the store

49. In the 1950s, families that were lucky enough to have a TV had three or four channels to choose from, <u>although todays' families may have three or four TVs and hundreds of channel choices.</u>
   a. although todays' families may have three or four TVs and hundreds of channel choices.
   b. while todays' families may have three or four TVs and hundreds of channel choices.
   c. however, today, there are families with three or four TVs and over a hundred channels that they can choose from.
   d. families today may have three or four TVs and hundreds of channels on them.
   e. although for todays' families, there may be three or four TVs and hundreds of channel choices.

50. <u>After the game was over,</u> the baseball coach handed out awards of one kind or another to each one of the players.
   a. After the game was over,
   b. Although the game was over,
   c. Yet the game was over,
   d. Furthermore the game was over,
   e. But the game was over,

51. <u>If one has such a terrible headache,</u> you can go and see my chiropractor and see if he can help you!
   a. If one has such a terrible headache
   b. If you has such a terrible headache
   c. If one had such a terrible headache
   d. If you have such a terrible headache
   e. If one was having a terrible headache

52. <u>The third-grade class went to visit</u> the community retirement center on Valentine's Day, and everyone there wanted to know where we went to school.
   a. The third-grade class went to visit
   b. That third-grade class went to visit
   c. Our third-grade class went to visit
   d. Her third-grade class went to visit
   e. Their third-grade class went to visit

53. Allen was shocked to find the money he had been missing looking through multiple loads of his dirty laundry.

    a. Allen was shocked to find the money he had been missing looking through multiple loads of his dirty laundry.

    b. Shocked, Allen found the money he had been missing looking through multiple loads of his dirty laundry.

    c. Looking through multiple loads of dirty laundry, the money Allen had been missing shocked him.

    d. Looking through multiple loads of dirty laundry, Allen was shocked to find the money he had been missing.

    e. Allen, looking through multiple loads of his dirty laundry, was shocked to find the money he had been missing.

54. In order to find their way through the darkness, bats must use a system of sound waves called echolocation; they send out a cry that bounces back off surfaces where there are objects in front of them.

    a. where there are objects in front of them.

    b. indicating where there are objects in front of them.

    c. which are objects that might be in front of them.

    d. objects are there in front.

    e. that are in front of them.

55. Never clearly captured on a photograph or film of any kind, the group of experts met at the annual conference to discuss if Sasquatch was actually reality or just a delusion.

    a. Never clearly captured on a photograph or film of any kind, the group of experts met at the annual conference to discuss if Sasquatch was actually reality or just a delusion.

    b. At the annual conference, the group of experts met to discuss if Sasquatch was actually reality or just a delusion with ever being clearly captured on a photograph or film of any kind.

    c. Whether or not Sasquatch was actually reality of just a delusion, experts met at the annual conference to discuss because he had never been clearly captured on a photograph or film of any kind.

    d. The group of experts met at the annual conference to discuss if Sasquatch was actually reality or just a delusion since his image had never been clearly captured on a photograph or film of any kind.

    e. Whether actually reality or just a delusion, the experts met at the annual conference to discuss Sasquatch since he had never been clearly captured on a photograph or film of any kind.

56. The cabin was located several blocks from the oceanfront, <u>yet we could still hear the surf as we went to bed each night.</u>
- **a.** yet we could still hear the surf as we went to bed each night.
- **b.** we could still hear the surf as we went to bed each night.
- **c.** yet we could still hear the surf as they went to bed each night.
- **d.** but you could still hear the surf as they went to bed each night.
- **e.** yet we could still hear it as we went to bed each night.

57. The brand-new computer system at Maryann's house is both <u>more powerful and much faster than Joshua's house.</u>
- **a.** more powerful and much faster than Joshua's house.
- **b.** more powerful and much faster than Joshua.
- **c.** more powerful and much faster than Joshua's.
- **d.** more powerful and much faster than the computer at Joshua's house.
- **e.** more powerful and much faster than the one found in Joshua's house.

58. <u>After a relaxing soothing massage</u>, I wanted nothing more than to go home and sleep for the rest of the afternoon.
- **a.** After a relaxing soothing massage
- **b.** After a relaxing, soothing massage
- **c.** After a relaxing but soothing massage
- **d.** After a relaxing, although soothing massage
- **e.** After a relaxing, however, soothing massage

59. <u>Although she had handed out more than 100 petitions,</u> Corrine still did not have enough signatures to stop the department store from building in her city.
- **a.** Although she had handed out more than 100 petitions,
- **b.** Because she had handed out more than 100 petitions,
- **c.** Since she had handed out more than 100 hundred petitions,
- **d.** Whenever she had handed out more than 100 petitions,
- **e.** She had handed out more than 100 petitions,

60. Despite her best efforts, <u>the gourmet meal did not turn out near as glamorous and delicious</u> as Samantha had initially planned.
- **a.** the gourmet meal did not turn out near as glamorous and delicious
- **b.** the gourmet meal did not turn out near as glamorously and deliciously
- **c.** the gourmet meal did not turn out nearly as glamorously and deliciously
- **d.** the gourmet meal did not turn out nearly as glamorous and delicious
- **e.** the gourmet meal did not, nearly as glamorous and delicious, turn out

61. Every few years, vampires seem to come back into fashion, books, movies, and television shows cast the bloodsucker as the romantic hero almost every single time.
  a. into fashion, books, movies, and television shows
  b. into fashion, books movies, and television shows
  c. into fashion; books; movies, and television shows
  d. into fashion, yet books, movies, and television shows
  e. into fashion; books, movies, and television shows

62. Although Antonio Banderas is primarily known as an actor, his ability to sing, as seen in the well-known musical *Evita.*
  a. Although Antonio Banderas is primarily known as an actor, his ability to sing, as he demonstrated in the well-known musical *Evita.*
  b. Although Antonio Banderas is primarily known as an actor, as he demonstrated in the well-known musical *Evita,* his ability to sing.
  c. Although Antonio Banderas is primarily known as an actor, he is also recognized for his ability sing, as he demonstrated in the well-known musical, *Evita.*
  d. Although Antonio Banderas is primarily known as an actor, he also an ability to sing, as he demonstrated in the well-known musical *Evita.*
  e. Although Antonio Banderas is primarily known as an actor, his ability to sing, as seen in the well-known musical *Evita,* is also known.

63. The Oregon coast offers tourists everything from soaring seagulls, roaring waves, towering mountains, and ocean water that is freezing.
  a. and ocean water that is freezing.
  b. and freezing ocean water.
  c. and water from the ocean that is freezing.
  d. plus ocean water freezing.
  e. and water that is freezing in the ocean.

64. Although television shows like *Friends, Seinfeld, Everybody Loves Raymond,* and *Frasier* are no longer being produced, yet people can still watch multiple episodes a day, thanks to cable television and reruns.
  a. yet people still can watch multiple episodes a day, thanks to cable television and reruns.
  b. although people can still watch multiple episodes a day, thanks to cable television and reruns.
  c. yet people can still watch multiple episodes a day; thanks to cable television and reruns.
  d. people can still watch multiple episodes a day, thanks to cable television and reruns.
  e. for people can still watch multiple episodes a day, thanks to cable television and reruns.

65. Although there are millions of people who avidly watch the Super Bowl each year, there are also millions who just as passionately run in the opposite direction and watch something else entirely.
  a. Although there are millions of people who avidly watch the Super Bowl each year,
  b. Because there are millions of people who avidly watch the Super Bowl each year,
  c. That there are also millions of people who avidly watch the Super Bowl each year,
  d. Avidly watching the Super Bowl each year, there are millions of people,
  e. There are millions of people who avidly watch the Super Bowl each year,

66. <u>Since entire seasons of television shows are now being released on DVD,</u> so people can enjoy their favorite shows or discover new ones completely free of commercial interruptions.
   a. Since entire seasons of television shows are now being released on DVD,
   b. Although entire seasons of television shows are now being released on DVD,
   c. Entire seasons of television shows, since are now being released on DVD,
   d. Because entire seasons of television shows are now being released on DVD,
   e. Entire seasons of television shows are now being released on DVD,

67. Alternative therapies like massage, acupuncture, hypnotherapy, and homeopathy are slowly <u>growing in popularity people are constantly looking</u> for new answers to old problems.
   a. growing in popularity people are constantly looking
   b. growing in popularity, people are constantly looking
   c. growing in popularity; people are constantly looking
   d. growing in popularity although people are constantly looking
   e. growing in popularity, people is constantly looking

68. The new hair salon offers a multitude of services including massages, pedicures, manicures, mud baths, and <u>you can get your hair cut and styled, too.</u>
   a. you can get your hair cut and styled, too.
   b. one can get their hair cut and styled, too.
   c. hair cuts and styles, too.
   d. your hair cut and styled, too.
   e. as well as hair cuts and styles.

69. <u>To play the guitar good,</u> you have to develop calluses on your fingertips, cut your nails short, learn to read music, and understand how to clearly produce multiple chords.
   a. To play the guitar good,
   b. To play the guitar goodly,
   c. To have played the guitar good,
   d. To play the guitar well,
   e. To playing the guitar well,

70. <u>Lionel wrote a science-fiction story where the aliens,</u> who came from a planet no one even knew existed before, are not hostile or destructive but benevolent and kind instead.
   a. Lionel wrote a science-fiction story where the aliens
   b. Lionel is writing a science-fiction story but the aliens
   c. Lionel wrote a science-fiction story, although the aliens
   d. Lionel is writing a science-fiction story, the aliens
   e. Lionel wrote a science-fiction story in which the aliens

71. <u>If you deeply appreciate books</u> with unbelievable descriptions and amazing metaphors, you definitely have to read anything you possibly can by science fiction author Ray Bradbury.
   a. If you deeply appreciate books
   b. If one deeply appreciates books
   c. If they deeply appreciate books
   d. If we deeply appreciate books
   e. If he deeply appreciates books

72. Although voice lessons help increase a chance of being chosen for a part in the community play, <u>they look at other elements</u>, including appearance, confidence, range and enunciation.
  a. they look at other elements
  b. the casting committee looks at other elements
  c. yet they look at other elements
  d. the casting committee looks at other elements
  e. yet they are looking at other elements

73. The horrors of war, described in detail in the classic *Red Badge of Courage*, are painful and difficult to read, <u>yet just as true today as they were hundreds of years ago.</u>
  a. yet just as true today as they were hundreds of years ago.
  b. since just as true today as they were hundreds of years ago.
  c. just as true today as they were hundreds of years ago.
  d. because just as true today as they were hundreds of years ago.
  e. for just as true today as they were hundreds of years ago.

74. Allison is definitely the best person to lead <u>our group, she is confident</u>, intelligent, knowledgeable, and considerate.
  a. our group, she is confident
  b. our group, because she is confident
  c. our group, confident she is
  d. our group, although she is confident
  e. our group; for she is confident

75. When I read through the list of driving rules and regulations, <u>it was amazing how many mistakes you could make without even knowing it.</u>
  a. it was amazing how many mistakes you could make without even knowing it.
  b. it was amazing how many mistakes they could make without even knowing it.
  c. it was amazing how many mistakes I could make without even knowing it.
  d. it was amazing how many mistakes one could make without even knowing it.
  e. it was amazing how many mistakes we could make without even knowing it.

76. The parents looked at their high school graduate <u>so proud</u> that they almost seemed to glow with happiness.
  a. so proud
  b. so very proud
  c. so prideful
  d. so proudly
  e. so much pride

77. To the disappointment of the audience, <u>neither Hank Azaria nor Tim Curry were going</u> to be in that night's performance of *Spamalot*.
  a. neither Hank Azaria nor Tim Curry were going
  b. neither Hank Azaria nor Tim Curry are going
  c. neither Hank Azaria or Tim Curry was going
  d. neither Hank Azaria nor Tim Curry go
  e. neither Hank Azaria nor Tim Curry was going

78. Considering that he had already eaten three pieces of pizza, a bag of potato chips, four apples, and a few pretzels, I think the college student should not have guzzled the liter of soda <u>as quick as he did</u>.
   a. as quick as he did
   b. as very quick as he is doing
   c. as extremely quick as he did
   d. as quickly as he did
   e. as quickly as he is doing

79. If you are more than 15 minutes late to work, you will get a penalty <u>and one may only have two of these penalties per month or you will be fired.</u>
   a. and one may only have two of these penalties per month or you will be fired.
   b. and one may only have two of these penalties per month or one will be fired.
   c. and you may only have two of these penalties per month or you will be fired.
   d. and you may only have two of these penalties per month or they will be fired.
   e. and you may only have two of these penalties per month or we will be fired.

80. To the brand-new mother, <u>every baby in the hospital nursery are beautiful</u>, none so much, of course, as her very own.
   a. every baby in the hospital nursery are beautiful
   b. every baby in the hospital nursery is beautiful
   c. every baby in the hospital nurseries is beautiful
   d. every babies in the hospital nurseries are beautiful
   e. every baby in the hospital nursery must be beautiful

81. <u>Because she was up in her room with her head-phones on</u>, Jennifer never even heard the doorbell ringing downstairs.
   a. Because she was up in her room with her headphones on
   b. She was up in her room with her headphones on
   c. Although she was in her room with her headphones on
   d. She was up in her room and her headphones were on
   e. Because her headphones were on up in her room

82. <u>Held in 1927, President Calvin Coolidge presided over the ceremony to officially commence the carving of Mount Rushmore.</u>
   a. Held in 1927, President Calvin Coolidge presided over the ceremony to officially commence the carving of Mount Rushmore.
   b. Held in 1927, it was President Calvin Coolidge who presided over the ceremony to officially commence the carving of Mount Rushmore.
   c. The carving of Mount Rushmore was officially commenced in 1927, at a cermony that was presided over by President Calvin Coolidge.
   d. President Calvin Coolidge presided over the 1927 ceremony that officially commenced the carving of Mount Rushmore.
   e. The 1927 ceremony, presided over by President Calvin Coolidge, which officially commenced the carving of Mount Rushmore.

83. <u>Six cases of canned peaches were taken out of the grocery store that were dented and way past their expiration date.</u>

  a. Six cases of canned peaches were taken out of the grocery store that were dented and way past their expiration date.

  b. Six cases of canned peaches way past their expiration date were taken out of the grocery store and they were dented.

  c. Six cases of canned peaches that were dented and past their expiration date were taken out of the grocery store.

  d. Dented and past their expiration date, the grocery store took out six cases of canned peaches.

  e. The grocery store took out the peaches that were dented plus they were way past their expiration date.

84. The country fair judges award the first prize to the cherry pie that has the flakiest crust, the sweetest cherries, <u>and how it tastes best overall.</u>

  a. and how it tastes best overall.

  b. and tasting it best overall.

  c. how it tastes best overall.

  d. and the best overall taste.

  e. and its best overall tastiest.

85. Musical artists, such as the Rolling Stones, They Might Be Giants, and Coldplay, <u>regular tours the country,</u> and at their concerts, you can buy programs, hats, T-shirts, and CDs.

  a. regular tours the country

  b. regularly touring the country

  c. regular tour the country

  d. regularly tour the country

  e. regular tours of the country

86. The football team ran out onto the field and got into position; <u>each player knew exactly where they were supposed to go,</u> thanks to all of those hours of practice.

  a. each player knew exactly where they were supposed to go

  b. each player knowing exactly where they were supposed to go

  c. each player knew exactly where he was supposed to go

  d. each player knew exactly where one was supposed to go

  e. each one of the players knowing exactly where to go

87. Although a high GPA and solid SAT scores can enhance your school transcript, <u>they frequently look beyond the numbers</u> to how you spend your spare time.
a. they frequently look beyond the numbers
b. college admission reps frequently look beyond the numbers
c. the people from different colleges frequently look beyond the numbers
d. they frequent look beyond the numbers
e. looking beyond the numbers college admission reps do

88. The sprinkler out in the middle of the golf course <u>was malfunctioning; water was coming out</u>, but the sprinkler itself was not moving a single inch.
a. was malfunctioning; water was coming out
b. was malfunctioning, water was coming out
c. was malfunctioning water was coming out
d. was malfunctioning although water was coming out
e. was malfunctioning but water was coming out

89. According to the weather report, <u>there are three thunderstorms in the area and if they connect,</u> it is going to be an extremely powerful system.
a. there are three thunderstorms in the area and if they connect,
b. there is three thunderstorms in the area and if they connect,
c. there are three thunderstorms in the area and if they connected,
d. there is three thunderstorms in the area and if they are connecting
e. three thunderstorms are in the area and they're connecting

90. The metric system, originally adopted in France after the French Revolution in 1789, <u>has still not caught up in the United States</u>.
a. has still not caught up in the United States
b. has still not caught at in the United States
c. has still not caught in the United States
d. has still not caught from in the United States
e. has still not caught on in the United States

91. <u>Although computers are considered to be a modern invention</u>, historical records show that English mathematician Charles Babbage invented the first official computer in the 1800s; he called it the Analytical Machine.
a. Although computers are considered to be a modern invention
b. Because computers are considered to be a modern invention
c. Since computers are considered to be a modern invention
d. Computers are considered to be a modern invention
e. Computers, considered to be a modern invention,

92. <u>Scientists have been working through the clock</u> trying to figure out if the multiple mysterious objects hovering around Jupiter are actually asteroids or comets.
a. Scientists have been working through the clock
b. Scientists have been working under the clock
c. Scientists have been working around the clock
d. Scientists have been working over the clock
e. Scientists have been working the clock

93. While history cannot prove that Isaac Newton really had an apple fall on his head, <u>yet he certainly was an influential scientist</u> in exploring exactly how gravity works.
   a. yet he certainly was an influential scientist
   b. but he certainly was an influential scientist
   c. because he certainly was an influential scientist
   d. he certainly was an influential scientist
   e. although he certainly was an influential scientist

94. During the field trip to the Smithsonian Institute, the museum's <u>displays that were like a time travel machine</u>, allowing us all the chance to glimpse the past.
   a. displays that were like a time travel machine
   b. displays were like a time travel machine
   c. displaying that were like a time travel machine
   d. displays that was like a time travel machine
   e. display were like a time travel machine

95. <u>When Katherine went online to get the concert tickets;</u> she was horrified to find out that the performance had already been completely sold out.
   a. When Katherine went online to get the concert tickets;
   b. When Katherine went online to get the concert tickets
   c. Katherine went online to get the concert tickets,
   d. Katherine, going online to get the concert tickets,
   e. When Katherine went online to get the concert tickets,

96. The zipper was not invented until 1891 by a <u>man named Whitcomb Judson until then, people used buttons,</u> hooks, and pins to keep their clothing together.
   a. man named Whitcomb Judson until then, people used buttons,
   b. man named Whitcomb Judson, until then, people used buttons,
   c. man named Whitcomb Judson since, until then, people used buttons,
   d. man named Whitcomb Judson; until then, people used buttons,
   e. man named Whitcomb Judson, while, until then, people used buttons,

97. <u>Melanie was visiting her cousins in New Jersey and there was a mild earthquake in her California hometown.</u>
   a. Melanie was visiting her cousins in New Jersey and there was a mild earthquake in her California hometown.
   b. Melanie was visiting her cousins in New Jersey, but there was a mild earthquake in her California hometown.
   c. While Melanie was visiting her cousins in New Jersey, there was a mild earthquake in her California hometown.
   d. Although Melanie was visiting her cousins in New Jersey, there was a mild earthquake in her California hometown.
   e. Because Melanie was visiting her cousins in New Jersey, there was a mild earthquake in her California hometown.

98. When Howard went to the emergency room with a potential heart attack, <u>the medical team looked carefully at his heart rate, his breathing, what his blood oxygen levels were, and his overall coherency.</u>
  a. the medical team looked carefully at his heart rate, his breathing, what his blood oxygen levels were, and his overall coherency.
  b. the medical team looked carefully at his heart rate, breathing, blood oxygen levels, and overall coherency.
  c. the medical team looked carefully at his heart rate, his breathing, what his blood oxygen levels were, and how his overall coherency was.
  d. the medical team looked carefully at his heart rate, breathing, blood oxygen levels, and his overall coherency.
  e. the medical team looked carefully at his heart rate, his breathing, what his blood oxygen levels were, as well as his overall coherency.

99. <u>Because she had been absent for the first two weeks of physics class,</u> Cordelia did far worse on the midterm exam than she had hoped.
  a. Because she had been absent for the first two weeks of physics class,
  b. Although she had been absent for the first two weeks of physics class,
  c. While she had been absent for the first two weeks of physics class,
  d. She had been absent for the first two weeks of physics class,
  e. When she had been absent for the first two weeks of physics class,

100. <u>Carmen waited as the glittering crown was placed on her head, having won first place in the beauty pageant.</u>
  a. Carmen waited as the glittering crown was placed on her head, having won first place in the beauty pageant.
  b. Carmen waited as the glittering crown was placed on her head, winning first place in the beauty pageant.
  c. Having won first place in the beauty pageant, Carmen waited as the glittering crown was placed on her head.
  d. Carmen waited, having won first place in the beauty pageant, as the glittering crown was placed on her head.
  e. Having won first places in the beauty pageant, the glittering crown was placed on Carmen's head.

101. <u>Though you are going to visit New York City,</u> you simply must stop by the Empire State Building and see one of the most amazing viewpoints in the entire city.
  a. Though you are going to visit New York City,
  b. Unless you are going to visit New York City,
  c. Whether you are going to visit New York City,
  d. If you are going to visit New York City,
  e. Before you are going to visit New York City,

102. Under the kitchen cupboard, there <u>is one spray bottle of window cleaner and two brand-new sponges that</u> you can use to clean the bathroom.
   a. is one spray bottle of window cleaner and two brand-new sponges that
   b. a spray bottle of window cleaner and two brand-new sponges which
   c. you will find a spray bottle of window cleaner and two brand-new sponges that
   d. are one spray bottle of window cleaner and two brand-new sponges who
   e. are one spray bottle of window cleaner and two brand-new sponges that

103. Some coaches believe that the primary goal for <u>participation in professional sports has changed over the years from enjoyment to financial gain.</u>
   a. participation in professional sports has changed over the years from enjoyment to financial gain.
   b. participation in professional sports have changed over the years from enjoyment to financial gain.
   c. participating in professional sports has changed over the years from enjoyment to financial gain.
   d. participate in professional sports has changed over the years from enjoyment to financial gain.
   e. participation in professional sports have changing over the years from enjoyment to financial gain.

104. Sarita, in the Girl Scout cookie booth next to the bank, <u>selling Thin Mints for the last three hours.</u>
   a. selling Thin Mints for the last three hours.
   b. has been selling Thin Mints for the last three hours.
   c. Thin Mints, for the last three hours selling.
   d. for the last three hours, selling Thin Mints.
   e. have been selling Thin Mints for the last three hours.

105. If you want to listen to your music at that volume, you will have to understand that <u>you will be expected to keep their door closed.</u>
   a. you will be expected to keep their door closed.
   b. they will be expected to keep your door closed.
   c. you will be expected to keep your door closed.
   d. you are expecting to keep your door closed.
   e. he will be expected to keep your door closed.

106. <u>Both my brothers who live in Acapulco</u> have jobs in the computer field.
   a. Both my brothers who live in Acapulco
   b. Both of my two brothers who live in Acapulco
   c. My brothers, both who live in Acapulco,
   d. My two brothers in Acapulco
   e. My two brothers, living in Acapulco,

107. <u>This week's basketball practice was missed</u> because we had a dentist's appointment that we had to keep.

    a. This week's basketball practice was missed

    b. We missed this week's basketball practice

    c. This week's basketball practice we missed

    d. We missed the basketball practice that was this week

    e. Basketball practice this week was missed

108. Occasionally, singers like Phil Collins and Rob Thomas will <u>leave their bands, go out on their own</u>, and succeed beyond anyone's expectations.

    a. leave their bands, go out on their own

    b. leave your bands, go out on other own

    c. leave his bands, go out on his own

    d. leave her bands, go out on her own

    e. leave our bands, go out on our own

109. According to the police report, it was abundantly clear to everyone involved that <u>the priceless diamond had been stoled sometime during the night.</u>

    a. the priceless diamond had been stoled sometime during the night.

    b. the priceless diamond had been stolen sometime during the night.

    c. the priceless diamond stolen sometime during the night.

    d. the priceless diamond stealed sometime during the night.

    e. the priceless diamond having been stolen sometime during the night.

110. Although Shawn was sure that the letter would come today, one look at his mother's face and <u>he knew he hadn't gotten no mail yet.</u>

    a. he knew he hadn't gotten no mail yet.

    b. he knew he had not gotten no mail yet.

    c. he knew he hadn't gotten any mail yet.

    d. he knew he hasn't gotten any mail yet.

    e. he knew he hadn't got no mail yet.

111. <u>The amazing piece of music that Victoria played during the climax of the entire orchestra concert.</u>

    a. The amazing piece of music that Victoria played during the climax of the entire orchestra concert.

    b. The amazing piece of music Victoria played during the climax of the entire orchestra concert.

    c. During the climax of the entire orchestra concert, an amazing piece of music was played by Victoria.

    d. Victoria played an amazing piece of music during the climax of the entire orchestra concert.

    e. Victoria, during the climax of the entire orchestra concert, an amazing piece of music she played.

112. Internet search engines are revolutionary in their capacity to provide a free service to users, <u>also offering targeted, low-key advertisements that assist users in their search.</u>

 a. also offering targeted, low-key advertise- ments that assist users in their search.

 b. while offering targeted, low-key advertise- ments that assist users in their search.

 c. while, offering advertisements that are low key and targeted to assist users in their search.

 d. while they offer targeted advertisements that are low key and assist users to find what they're looking for.

 e. as well as offering targeted, low-key advertisements to help users find things.

113. Some authors write a monumental best-seller and then never <u>write anything else, Harper Lee and Margaret Mitchell</u> are two perfect examples of this.

 a. write anything else, Harper Lee and Margaret Mitchell

 b. write anything else Harper Lee and Margaret Mitchell

 c. write anything else because Harper Lee and Margaret Mitchell

 d. write anything else; Harper Lee and Margaret Mitchell

 e. write anything else unless Harper Lee and Margaret Mitchell

114. The first interspecies transplant is believed to have been completed in the early 1800s, <u>when scientists grafted the tail of a rat onto the comb of a rooster.</u>

 a. when scientists grafted the tail of a rat onto the comb of a rooster.

 b. with the grafting of the tail of a rat onto the comb of a rooster by scientists.

 c. when scientists, with the tail of a rat, grafted it onto the comb of a rooster.

 d. scientists had grafted the tail of a rat onto the comb of a rooster.

 e. thus, the tail of a rat had been grafted onto a rooster's comb.

115. After spending the last four hours in the kitchen, <u>the gourmet meal was an incredible triumph for Melanie,</u> even if her mother-in- law didn't happen to agree.

 a. the gourmet meal was an incredible tri- umph for Melanie,

 b. Melanie's gourmet meal was an incredible triumph,

 c. an incredible triumph the gourmet meal was for Melanie,

 d. Melanie's incredible triumph was the gour- met meal

 e. the gourmet meal, an incredible triumph for Melanie,

116. <u>Although I had not wanted to attend the con-</u>
<u>cert</u>, I was soon covered in goose bumps as I
listened to the beautiful music soar through
the auditorium.

    a. Although I had not wanted to attend
the concert

    b. Unless I had not wanted to attend
the concert

    c. Because I had not wanted to attend
the concert

    d. After I had not wanted to attend the concert

    e. If I had not wanted to attend the concert

117. In order to receive the contest's grand prize,
<u>the winner must follow the rules closely; they</u>
<u>must write an essay</u> between 1,500 and 2,500
words long, and you have to center it on the
most viable solution to the ongoing problem
of world famine.

    a. the winner must follow the rules closely;
they must write an essay

    b. the winner must follow the rules closely; he
or she must write an essay

    c. the winner must follow the rules closely;
you must write an essay

    d. the winner must follow the rules closely; I
must write an essay

    e. the winner must follow the rules closely; we
must write an essay

118. The plastic surgeon anticipated <u>my every</u>
<u>question; he answered</u> every single one of
them before I could even put it into words.

    a. my every question; he answered

    b. my every question he answered

    c. my every question, he answered

    d. my every question until he answered

    e. my every question if he answered

119. According to the American Dental Society,
<u>there is many different reasons</u> that some peo-
ple are more prone to dental cavities than
other people.

    a. there is many different reasons

    b. there was many different reasons

    c. there will be many different reasons

    d. there is many differing reasons

    e. there are many different reasons

120. The family's collected photographs, cards, letters, and other memorabilia <u>fills the scrap-</u>
<u>book from the very first page to the last one.</u>

    a. fills the scrapbook from the very first page
to the last one.

    b. filling the scrapbook from the very first
page to the last one.

    c. did fills the scrapbook from the very first
page to the last one.

    d. fill the scrapbook from the very first page to
the last one.

    e. full of the scrapbook from the very first
page to the last one.

121. Wireless technology is changing so fast that
it often seems like whatever product you buy
is <u>already obsolete before one even leaves</u>
<u>the store.</u>

    a. already obsolete before one even leaves
the store.

    b. already obsolete before one even begins to
leave the store.

    c. already obsolete before you even leave
the store.

    d. already obsolete before we can even leave
the store.

    e. already obsolete before the customer even
leaves the store.

122. To clean out her van before she picked up her in-laws, Karen picked up all of the fast-food wrappers, put all the CDs back in their cases, piled up the miscellaneous library books, <u>and she is also washing each one of the windows.</u>
  a. and she is also washing each one of the windows.
  b. and washed each one of the windows.
  c. and washing each one of the windows.
  d. she also washed each one of the windows.
  e. and washes each one of the windows.

123. The new laptop was faster and more advanced technologically <u>than any computer I had ever seen.</u>
  a. than any computer I had ever seen.
  b. than any other computer I had ever seen.
  c. than any other computer I had ever saw.
  d. than any computer I has seen.
  e. than any other computer ever seen.

124. Although I had been thinking about nothing else for weeks, I still had not decided <u>whether to fly back to Indiana or take the train.</u>
  a. whether to fly back to Indiana or take the train.
  b. weather to fly back or take the train to Indiana.
  c. weather to fly back to Indiana or take the train.
  d. weather I should fly or take the train back to Indiana.
  e. whether flying back to Indiana to take the train.

125. Few young people today remember when the singer Prince temporarily decided to change his name to a symbol, causing late-night talk show hosts <u>to dub him "the artist formally known as Prince."</u>
  a. to dub him "the artist formally known as Prince."
  b. dubbing him "the artist formerly known as Prince."
  c. to dub him "the artist formerly known as Prince."
  d. dubs him "the artist formally known as Prince."
  e. dubbed him "the artist formerly known as Prince."

126. <u>According to the previews we watched before the movie started, that huge new blockbuster with Orlando Bloom will be opening in just a matter of weeks.</u>
  a. According to the previews we watched before the movie started, that huge new blockbuster with Orlando Bloom will be opening in just a matter of weeks.
  b. That huge new blockbuster with Orlando Bloom, in the previews we watched before the movie started, will be opening in just a matter of weeks.
  c. In just a matter of weeks, that huge new blockbuster with Orlando Bloom will be released, according to the previews which we watched before the movie started.
  d. Opening in just a matter of weeks is that huge new blockbuster with Orlando Bloom which was in the previews that we watched before the movie started in the previews.
  e. According to the previews that huge new blockbuster with Orlando Bloom will be opening in just a matter of weeks it said before the movie started.

127. Margaret simply could not believe it <u>when she was asked to join the city council;</u> she had been waiting for an opportunity like this for years.
- **a.** when she was asked to join the city council;
- **b.** when she was asking to join the city council;
- **c.** when she was asked to join the city counsel;
- **d.** when she was asked to join the city consul;
- **e.** when she was being asked to join the city council;

128. It was so cold in the house that the kids were shocked to discover <u>that they could see their own breathe.</u>
- **a.** that they could see their own breathe.
- **b.** they you could see their own breath.
- **c.** that their own breathe they could see.
- **d.** seeing their own breath, they could.
- **e.** that they could see their own breath.

129. While the vast majority of accountants would advise their clients to prepare their federal income taxes by the end of February, <u>a sizable portion of people</u> until the very last possible minute.
- **a.** a sizable portion of people
- **b.** a sizable portion of most people
- **c.** a sizable portion of people wait
- **d.** a sizable portion of people waiting
- **e.** a sizable portion of people waits

130. Although many people know that Meg Ryan and Tom Hanks starred together in *You've Got Mail* and *Sleepless in Seattle*, <u>few seem to remember that they were also together in *Joe versus the Volcano.*</u>
- **a.** few seem to remember that they were also together in *Joe versus the Volcano.*
- **b.** few are remembering that they were also together in *Joe versus the Volcano.*
- **c.** few remembered that they were also together in *Joe versus the Volcano.*
- **d.** few seem to be remembering that they were also together in *Joe versus the Volcano.*
- **e.** few seemingly remember that they were also together in *Joe versus the Volcano.*

131. <u>Until we get an unbelievably fast and knowledgeable cab driver</u>, we will never be able to make our plane departure on time.
- **a.** Until we get an unbelievably fast and knowledgeable cab driver
- **b.** Although we get an unbelievable fast and knowledgeable cab driver
- **c.** Since we get an unbelievably fast and knowledgeable cab driver
- **d.** When we get an unbelievably fast and knowledgeable cab driver
- **e.** Whether we get an unbelievably fast and knowledgeable cab driver

132. <u>After shopping at the mall for five hours nonstop, the plush chair felt amazingly soft and welcoming to Megan's tired legs.</u>
   a. After shopping at the mall for five hours nonstop, the plush chair felt amazingly soft and welcoming to Megan's tired legs.
   b. Shopping at the mall for five hours nonstop, the plush chair felt amazingly soft and welcoming to Megan's tired legs.
   c. Megan's legs were tired, and after shopping for five hours nonstop, the plush chair felt amazingly soft and welcoming to them.
   d. The plush chair felt amazingly soft and welcome to Megan's tired legs after she had been shopping at the mall for five hours nonstop.
   e. After shopping at the mall for five hours nonstop, Megan thought that the plush chair felt amazingly soft and welcoming to her tired legs.

133. The Little League baseball team has decided to postpone their annual car wash <u>because the rainy season officially comes to an end.</u>
   a. because the rainy season officially comes to an end.
   b. before the rainy season officially comes to an end.
   c. until the rainy season officially comes to an end.
   d. although the rainy season officially comes to an end.
   e. whereas the rainy season officially comes to an end.

134. Despite the incredibly inclement weather, <u>my parents and I drove all the way back from the coast;</u> we fortunately arrived home safely in plenty of time for me to get to work.
   a. my parents and I drove all the way back from the coast;
   b. my parents and I drived all the way back from the coast;
   c. my parents and I are driving all the way back from the coast;
   d. my parents and I driven all the way back from the coast;
   e. my parents and I have been driven all the way back from the coast;

135. <u>Having kicked her door shut, Caroline felt terribly disappointed about not getting a car for her birthday.</u>
   a. Having kicked her door shut, Caroline felt terribly disappointed about not getting a car for her birthday.
   b. Terribly disappointed about not getting a car for her birthday, Caroline kicked her door shut.
   c. Kicking her door shut, terribly disappointed about not getting a car for her birthday was Caroline.
   d. Caroline didn't get a car for her birthday, therefore, she kicked her door shut as she was terribly disappointed.
   e. Not getting a car for her birthday, the door was kicked shut by a terribly disappointed Caroline.

136. Human beings are taller and stronger than 200 years ago; since 1800, the average adult height has increased by 18 inches.

    a. Human beings are taller and stronger than 200 years ago;

    b. Human being's are taller and stronger than 200 years ago,

    c. Humans, being taller and stronger than they were 200 years ago;

    d. Human beings are taller and stronger than they were 200 years ago;

    e. Being taller and stronger than 200 years ago,

137. Martin found that science class was hardest during the senior year, just like Carson.

    a. Martin found that science class was hardest during the senior year, just like Carson.

    b. Like Carson, Martin found that science class was hardest during the senior year.

    c. Martin found that science class was hardest during the senior year, just like Carson did.

    d. Science class was the hardest during the senior year is what Martin and Carson found.

    e. Senior year science class was hardest as found out by both Martin and Carson.

138. For decades, the mystery has continued to baffle young people; if Pluto is a dog, what in the world is Goofy?

    a. young people; if Pluto is a dog

    b. young people, if Pluto is a dog

    c. young people if Pluto is a dog

    d. young people and if Pluto is a dog

    e. young people because if Pluto is a dog

139. Lydia suddenly realized that the reason her car was not working was it didn't have no gas left in it.

    a. it didn't have no gas left in it.

    b. it did not have no gas left in it.

    c. it does not have no gas left in it.

    d. it do not have any gas left in it.

    e. it didn't have any gas left in it.

140. The world has seen the rise and demise of record albums, eight-track tapes, and cassette tapes, one has to wonder what will follow compact discs.

    a. cassette tapes, one has to wonder

    b. cassette tapes one has to wonder

    c. cassette tapes, one certainly has to wonder

    d. cassette tapes; one has to wonder

    e. cassette tapes since one has to wonder

141. <u>Driving for the first time, the traffic intimi-dated the teenager and she worried about keeping track of the cars behind and in front of her.</u>
- **a.** Driving for the first time, the traffic intimi-dated the teenager and she worried about keeping track of the cars behind and in front of her.
- **b.** Driving for the first time, the teenager was intimidated by the traffic and worried about keeping track of the cars behind and in front of her.
- **c.** Driving for the first time and intimidated by the traffic, the cars behind and in front of the teenager worried her.
- **d.** The teenager was intimidated by the traffic as she was driving for the first time and keeping track of the cars behind and in front of her worried her.
- **e.** The traffic intimidated the teenager and she worried about keeping track of the cars behind and in front of her since she was driving for the first time.

142. No matter how hard I concentrated on the test question, <u>the solution to it kept alluding me.</u>
- **a.** the solution to it kept alluding me.
- **b.** alluding me was the solution to it.
- **c.** the solution was keeping allusive.
- **d.** the solution was kept elusive.
- **e.** the solution to it kept eluding me.

143. The vineyards of southern California are at once breathlessly vibrant, obsessively symmet-rical, <u>and the green is profound.</u>
- **a.** and the green is profound.
- **b.** and its green is quite profound.
- **c.** and profoundly green.
- **d.** and it is profoundly green.
- **e.** and so profound green.

144. <u>Because you missed the college orientation meeting,</u> the first week on campus might be somewhat confusing for you.
- **a.** Because you missed the college orientation meeting,
- **b.** Although you missed the college orientation meeting,
- **c.** Until you missed the college orientation meeting,
- **d.** While you missed the college orientation meeting,
- **e.** Though you missed the college orientation meeting,

145. Because the position did not have all of the necessary job requirements, <u>so Marcus politely declined the offer.</u>
- **a.** so Marcus politely declined the offer.
- **b.** but Marcus was politely declining the offer.
- **c.** and this resulted in Marcus politely declining the offer.
- **d.** Marcus politely declined the offer.
- **e.** and Marcus politely declined the offer.

146. Although Patricia had been raised on a quiet, little farm far out in the country, she longed for a time somewhere in the future when her residence would be situated <u>right in the middle of a loud, bustling, hectic city.</u>

    a. right in the middle of a loud, bustling, hectic city.

    b. right in the middle of a loud and bustling and hectic city.

    c. right in the middle of a loud bustling hectic city.

    d. right in the middle of a loud, yet bustling and hectic city.

    e. right in the middle of a loud, although bustling, hectic city.

147. <u>When you do research on the Internet</u>, it is important that you evaluate each site critically; you need to consider the date of the information, the reliability of the author, and the accuracy of the facts.

    a. When you do research on the Internet

    b. When you did your research on the Internet

    c. When you have done your research on the Internet

    d. When you had done your research on the Internet

    e. When you will do your research on the Internet

148. There are many struggling authors in the world and <u>the fastest way for them to become millionaires is to have your book recommended</u> on the *Oprah* show.

    a. the fastest way for them to become millionaires is to have your book recommended

    b. the fastest way for them to become millionaires is to have their book recommended

    c. the fastest way for you to become a millionaire is to have your book recommended

    d. the fastest way for anyone to become a millionaire is to have your book recommended

    e. the fastest way for us to become millionaires is to have our book recommended

149. If one is sincerely interested in eventually earning a position in the community orchestra, <u>then they must practice on a regular basis</u> and play more with passion than with obligation.

    a. then they must practice on a regular basis

    b. then he or she must practice on a regular basis

    c. then we must practice on a regular basis

    d. then you must practice on regular basis

    e. then they must practice on a regularly basis

150. Although some believe that life is guided primarily by a predetermined destiny, <u>others completely convinced that each individual decision changes fate on a daily basis.</u>

  a. others completely convinced that each individual decision changes fate on a daily basis.
  b. others, completely convinced that each individual decision changes fate, on a daily basis.
  c. others are completely convinced that each individual decision changes fate on a day basis.
  d. others are completely convinced that each individual decision changes fate on a daily basis.
  e. others are completely convincing that each individual decisions changes fate on a daily basis.

151. The death of Coretta Scott King touched the <u>hearts of millions her strength and courage</u> after the death of her husband in 1968 was inspiring to many.

  a. hearts of millions her strength and courage
  b. hearts of millions, her strength and courage
  c. hearts of millions until her strength and courage
  d. hearts of millions although her strength and courage
  e. hearts of millions; her strength and courage

152. <u>Going to college can lead to some fantastic careers</u>, young adults who do not pursue additional education can also find extremely fulfilling and exciting professions as well.

  a. Going to college can lead to some fantastic careers
  b. Although going to college can lead to some fantastic careers
  c. Since going to college can lead to some fantastic careers
  d. If going to college can lead to some fantastic careers
  e. Unless going to college can lead to some fantastic careers

153. To Lana's disappointment, <u>the wedding plans weren't getting no easier</u> as her big day approached.

  a. the wedding plans weren't getting no easier
  b. the wedding plans wasn't getting any easier
  c. the wedding plans weren't getting any easier
  d. the wedding plans isn't getting any easier
  e. the wedding plans aren't getting no easier

154. The numereous side effects of chemotherapy are caused by the fact that the chemicals kill healthy cells as well as cancerous <u>cells, they are unable to distinguish</u> between the two.

  a. cells, they are unable to distinguish
  b. cells because unable to distinguish
  c. cells, which are unable to distinguish
  d. cells because the chemicals are unable to distinguish
  e. cells, which aren't distinguished

155. This summer will mark the fifth anniversary of us coming to live on Alberta Street in Farmington.
  a. of us coming to live on Alberta Street in Farmington.
  b. of we arriving on Alberta Street in Farmington.
  c. of we living on Alberta Street in Farmington.
  d. of us to come and live on Alberta Street in Farmington.
  e. of our coming to live on Alberta Street in Farmington.

156. During the fireworks, the colors that filled the sky like starbursts.
  a. the colors that filled the sky
  b. the colors filling the sky
  c. the colors filled the sky
  d. the colors, which filled the sky
  e. the colors will fill the sky

157. When choosing a sport, young people are encouraged to thoroughly consider how hard it is to learn, what kind of skills it takes, what equipment it requires, and its overall cost.
  a. its overall cost.
  b. how much it costs overall.
  c. if it costs money.
  d. the cost of it.
  e. the money needed for it.

158. The present was given to the newly married couple with the big, red satin bow wrapped around it.
  a. The present was given to the newly married couple with the big, red satin bow wrapped around it.
  b. The present that was given to the newly married couple with the big, red satin bow wrapped around it.
  c. The present, with the big, red satin bow wrapped around it, given to the newly married couple.
  d. The present with the big, red bow wrapped around it was given to the newly married couple.
  e. The newly married couple with the big, red satin bow wrapped around it was given the present.

159. "Bloody Sunday" refers to two different historical events: the 1905 massacre of hundreds of civilians engaged in a peaceful march in St. Petersburg, Russia, whereas in 1972, in Derry, Ireland, British soldiers killed 13 peaceful demonstrators.
  a. whereas in 1972, in Derry, Ireland, British soldiers killed 13 peaceful demonstrators.
  b. and the 1972 killing by British soldiers of 13 peaceful demonstrators in Derry, Ireland.
  c. but in 1972, there were 13 peaceful demonstrators killed by British soldiers in Derry, Ireland.
  d. in contrast, the 1972 killing by British soldiers of 13 peaceful demonstrators in Derry, Ireland.
  e. and in 1972, there was the killing by British soldiers of 13 people who were demonstrating peacefully in Derry, Ireland.

160. Although most of us would prefer to spend <u>spring break in Disneyland, we understand</u> that visiting our relatives in Montana is more important.
  a. spring break in Disneyland, we understand
  b. spring break in Disneyland; we understand
  c. spring break in Disneyland we understand
  d. spring break in Disneyland, but we understand
  e. spring break in Disneyland, until we understand

161. After learning the important lessons from more than 400 writing questions and essay prompts, <u>you will most likely be ready to take a break</u>.
  a. you will most likely be ready to take a break
  b. you will most likely be ready for taking a break
  c. you will most likely be ready to have taken a break
  d. you will most likely be readier to take a break
  e. you will most likely be readiest to take a break

▶ Answers

1. c. This is a sentence fragment because it is missing a verb. Only choice **c** adds the verb in the right tense.

2. e. The second part of this sentence is a fragment and is missing the complete verb. Choice **e** adds the verb *begin* to make it correct.

3. b. This is a run-on sentence with two independent clauses joined by a comma. The way to correct the error is to join the clauses with a semicolon as in choice **b**.

4. c. To correct this run-on sentence, you can turn the first independent clause into a dependent one. To do this successfully, however, you have to choose a subordinate conjunction (*although*) to show how the two sentences relate to each other. *Because* and *whenever* do not do this.

5. b. This is an example of a misplaced modifier. The introductory clause should modify the boys, not the couch.

6. e. This sentence contains faulty parallelism. All three verbs must be the same. The first two end in *-ing*, so the third one needs to be changed so that it does, too.

7. b. These two independent clauses are joined by a subordinate conjunction. Only *although* will

show the correct relationship between the two thoughts, however.

8. b. The dependent clause in the first half of this sentence does not have the right relationship to the second half. Only the addition of the word *although* connects the two halves.

9. e. You need to look at the relationship between the two independent clauses. The subordinate conjunction has to connect the clauses so that they make sense. Only the word *since* does this.

10. d. This is a run-on sentence that is best repaired by adding a semicolon. The conjunctions in the other examples do not show the relationship between the sentences correctly.

11. c. In the original form, the word *that* creates a dependent clause in the first part of the sentence. Putting the word *and* between the subject and verb makes the sentence confusing and incorrect. The best solution is to take any word in that position out, as in choice **c**.

12. e. Here is a run-on sentence. You can fix this problem by using the appropriate coordinating conjunction. In this case, the best one is the word *but*.

13. a. The original form is the best.

14. c. This is an example of a misplaced modifier. The introductory clause should modify the medication, not the physician.

15. b. The second part of this sentence is an independent clause, but it is missing a verb. Choice **b** adds the verb and maintains the subject-verb agreement.

16. d. This is an example of a run-on sentence, and adding a semicolon repairs the error. Inserting the conjunctions would change the meaning of the sentence.

17. c. In this sentence, the phrase *from the local high school history class* is modifying *student*, so it needs to be shifted without changing the meaning of the sentence.

18. a. The original form is the best.

19. e. The misplaced modifier at the beginning of the sentence should be moved so that it properly modifies *Kathleen and Kevin* instead of *ocean*.

20. a. The original form is the best.

21. d. Having both *couldn't* and *hardly* in this sentence creates a double negative. To best repair it, one of the negatives needs to be removed, as in choice **d**.

22. d. The word *that* turns the last half of the sentence into a dependent clause. Simply taking *that* out, as in choice **d**, makes this sentence complete and correct.

23. c. This is an example of a run-on sentence or two independent clauses with nothing to connect them. The insertion of the semicolon is the most common way to repair this error.

24. b. This is a comma splice, or a run-on sentence. The best and easiest repair for this type of error is the addition of a semicolon.

25. e. The second half of this sentence is a dependent clause, so the semicolon is not correct. A comma is needed instead.

26. b. This is an example of an independent clause followed by a dependent clause. A semicolon is not necessary. Only a comma is needed.

27. c. Here are two independent clauses that you need to connect correctly. In this case, a semicolon is the best option.

28. c. In this sentence, two independent clauses are connected by the conjunction *and*. Although grammatically correct, the two sentences relate to each other and require a conjunction that demonstrates that relationship. In this case, the best choice is the conjuction *although*.

29. e. This is an example of faulty parallelism. The first two examples are parallel in form, but the third one is not. Choice **e** corrects the error while retaining the overall meaning of the sentence.

30. b. This is an example of faulty parallelism. The first clause is written with the verb in the *-ing* form, and the verb—which is missing in the second clause—should match, as in choice **b**.

31. e. This sentence is confusing. In what order did things actually happen? You need to rearrange this sentence so that it makes more sense, as in choice **e**.

32. c. The way this sentence is written the bike appears to be wearing the shiny green pants. The sentence needs to be rearranged so that the modifiers are clearly describing the messenger, not the bike.

33. d. Here is an example of a misplaced modifier. It appears as if the icy roads are going to the concert. The sentence has to be rewritten to show that it was people who were headed to the concert instead.

34. c. This sentence shows a problem with verb tense. It switches in the middle of the sentence. To maintain consistency, the verb tenses must match. Choice **c** is the only option that matches the verb tenses.

35. e. Did you spot the pronoun shift in this sentence? The pronouns shift from *one* to *you*. To repair the error, the pronouns must be consistent. Only choice **e** does that.

36. b. This question tests subject-verb agreement. The subject is *option*, which is singular, so the verb must be singular, too.

37. e. The error here is faulty comparison. The sentence compares the two *Rush Hour* movies. Standard usage dictates that you include the word *other* with a comparison like this.

38. a. This is best in its original form.

39. e. *Conscience* is a moral awareness; *conscious* is a physical awareness. Josh was awake and physically aware of his environment.

40. b. When referring to people, you should use the word *who*. When referring to things, you can use the word *that*.

41. b. This sentence contains far too many unnecessary words. Choice **b** removes the most words while retaining the sentence's original meaning.

42. e. This sentence contains a double negative (*didn't* and *nothing*). One has to be changed or removed to make the sentence correct. Choice **e** does this.

43. d. This is a comma splice. Either a semicolon or a coordinating conjunction that shows the correct relationship between the two independent clauses can correct this error. Only choice **d** repairs the problem correctly.

44. a. This is best in its original form.

45. c. The error in this sentence is a pronoun shift. The sentence begins with *they* and changes to *one*. Choice **c** does the best job of making the pronouns consistent without changing the meaning of the sentence.

46. c. This sentence tests your ability to recognize a problem with verb tense. The first part of the sentence is in the past tense, and the second part is in the present tense. To maintain consistency, the verb in the underlined portion has to be put into the past tense.

47. b. This is a test of pronoun and antecedent agreement. The antecedent is *everyone*, which is singular, so the pronoun has to be singular, too. *Their* is plural, so it should be replaced with *his or her*, which is singular.

48. e. This sentence shifts from the active to the passive voice between the first and second clause. Only choice **e** puts the second clause into active voice, so it remains consistent.

49. b. In this choice, the suborninate conjunction *while* clearly and effectively expresses the right relationship between the two clauses. In choice **a**, *although* does not express the correct relationship. Choice **c**'s use of *however* is correct, but it is preceded by a comma instead of a semicolon, creating a run-on sentence. Choice **d** also creates a run-on sentence and does not offer a coordinating or subordinating conjunction to express the contrast between the two clauses. Choice **e** repeats the original error and adds unnecessary wordy constructions.

50. a. This sentence is best in its original form.

51. d. The pronoun agreement is incorrect in this sentence. It switches from *one* to *you*. To be consistent, the pronouns must match, so *one* should be changed to *you*.

52. c. This question tests pronoun/antecedent agreement. The last half of the sentence reads *we*, so that implies that the speaker had to be part of the third-grade class. The only pronoun that includes the speaker is *our*.

53. d. Here is a problem of misplaced modifiers. The sentence, as written, implies that money is able to look through laundry. The order of events is not quite clear because of the misplaced modifiers. Only choice **d** clarifies what actually happened.

54. e. This sentence is wordy and awkward. Cut it down to only the necessary words that still retain the sentence's original meaning.

55. d. The introductory clause is modifying *the group of experts* when it needs to modify *Sasquatch*.

56. a. The original form of the sentence is best.

57. d. This is an example of faulty comparison. You should be comparing the two computers, not a computer to a person or a house.

58. b. When there are two words modifying the same noun or verb, you need to put a comma between them. This shows that both of words are describing the same thing (*relaxing* and *soothing* both modify *massage*).

59. a. The original form of the sentence is best.

60. d. The word *near* is modifying *glamorous*, which makes it an adverb. To put *near* in adverb form, you need to add the *-ly* ending.

61. e. This is a comma splice error. A semicolon needs to be inserted between the two independent clauses. Be careful to retain the commas that separate the list of nouns, though.

62. c. This is a sentence fragment; it is missing a verb. Only choice **c** provides the verb without altering the sentence's original meaning.

63. b. Here, you must identify the faulty parallelism. The last phrase does not match the others; only choice **b** repairs this error.

64. d. The first part of this statement is a dependent clause, so it needs to be followed by an independent clause. Removing the conjunction (*yet*) makes the second part an independent clause.

65. a. The original form of the sentence is the best.

66. e. Because the second half of the sentence is a dependent clause (beginning with the conjunction *so*), the first half needs to be independent. That can be done by removing the word *since*.

67. c. This is a run-on sentence. The two independent clauses should be separated by either a semicolon or the correct conjunction. Choice **c** inserts the necessary semicolon.

68. c. This sentence contains a problem with faulty parallelism. *Massages, pedicures, manicures,*

mud baths is not parallel to *you can get your hair cut and styled, too.* The last example needs to be rewritten in noun form to match the previous examples.

69. d. This sentence contains an error in diction. Remember, adverbs modify active verbs. The correct word to modify *to play* is *well*, not *good*.

70. e. To fix this idiom error, the word *where* should be replaced with *in which.*

71. a. The original form of the sentence is the best.

72. b. *They* does not directly relate to any noun or pronoun in the sentence and needs to be clarified.

73. a. This sentence is best in its original form.

74. b. This is a comma splice, where two independent clauses are incorrectly connected by a comma. In this answer choice, the error is corrected by inserting the conjunction that shows the proper relationship between the clauses.

75. c. This sentence has a pronoun shift in it. It starts with *I* and then changes to *you.* Choice **c** makes both of the pronouns consistent.

76. d. The word *proud* needs to be an adverb, because it is modifying *looked. Proud* requires the *-ly* ending.

77. e. When you see the word *neither*, remember that you need to use *nor* (instead of *or*). Also, note that *neither* is singular, so you need a singular verb as well.

78. d. In this sentence, *quick* needs to be an adverb, because it is modifying *guzzled. Quick* requires the *-ly* ending.

79. c. This is another example of a pronoun shift. Pronoun usage must be consistent throughout the sentence.

80. b. In the underlined phrase, the subject is *baby*, which is singular, so the verb must be singular, too. *Are* should be changed to *is*, as in choice **b**.

81. a. This sentence is best in its original form.

82. d. Choice **a** has a misplaced modifier; it was the ceremony that was held in 1927, not President Coolidge. Choice **b** retains this error and adds a wordy construction. Choice **c** is grammatically correct but not as concise as choice **d** because it uses the passive voice. Choice **e** is a sentence fragment.

83. c. The way this sentence is written, it sounds as if the store was dented and past its expiration date. The sentence needs to be rewritten so that these details modify *canned peaches*.

84. d. This sentence has faulty parallelism. The last phrase, *and how it tastes best overall*, does not match the pattern of the others (*the flakiest crust, the sweetest cherries*). To make these phrases parallel, you need to change the last phrase to *and the best overall taste*.

85. d. This question tests subject-verb agreement. The subject is *artists*, which is plural, so the verb (*tour*) needs to match. Also, because *regular* is used as an adverb, it needs to keep the *-ly* ending.

86. c. In the underlined phrase, the subject is *player*, which is singular. The pronoun used is *they*, which is plural. Only choice **c** fixes the pronoun so it is consistent with the subject.

87. b. This is a case of an indefinite pronoun. The word *they* does not directly relate to any noun or pronoun in the sentence. Words need to be inserted to clarify who *they* are.

88. a. This sentence is best in its original form.

89. a. This sentence is best in its original form.

90. e. When the word *caught* is used, standard usage dictates that the phrase should be *caught on*, not *caught up*.

91. a. This sentence is best in its original form.

92. c. This is an idiomatic question. *Through the clock* is not the correct expression. Standard usage dictates that the expression to be used is *around the clock*.

93. d. This is an example of a dependent clause followed by another dependent clause. The second dependent clause has to be changed into an independent clause. The only way to do this is by removing the conjunction, as in choice **d**.

94. b. This is a sentence fragment. The word *that* turns an independent clause into a dependent one. The solution is to remove *that*.

95. e. A semicolon is used to connect two independent clauses. This sentence has a semicolon connecting an independent and a dependent clause, which is incorrect. You need to replace the semicolon with a comma.

96. d. This is an example of a run-on sentence. The insertion of the semicolon fixes the error. The conjunctions suggested in the other answer choices do not show the appropriate relationship between the clauses.

97. c. This is an example of faulty coordination. The two independent clauses do not seem to have any reasonable relationship to each other. The addition of the right connecting word (*while*) is essential.

98. b. This sentence is an example of faulty parallelism. *What his blood oxygen levels were* is not parallel to *his heart rate, his breathing*, and *his overall coherency*. Choice **b** makes them all parallel and eliminates the redundancy of *his*.

99. a. The sentence is best in its original form.

100. c. This is a case of faulty subordination. The relationship between the ideas is not clear or logical. In this example, the effect is presented before the cause, which causes confusion.

101. d. This is a case of faulty subordination. The subordinating conjunction at the beginning of this sentence is what determines the relationship between the ideas, so it must make sense. *Though* does not connect the ideas together logically. Another subordinating conjunction is needed.

102. e. This question tests subject-verb agreement. Because there are plural subjects in this sentence (*bottle* and *sponges*), the verb needs to be plural, too. Remember, when the subjects are things, *which* and *who* are not used. Rather, the word *that* should be applied.

103. a. This sentence is best in its original form.

104. b. This is an example of a faulty verb form. With an irregular verb like *to sell*, a helping verb has to be added and the correct verb tense (the past) must be maintained.

105. c. This sentence contains a pronoun error. Because *you* and *your* are used throughout the sentence, *their* is incorrect in the underlined section.

106. d. Although this sentence is grammatically correct, it is redundant and wordy. By cutting out the unnecessary words while retaining the sentence's original meaning, you can fix this problem, as shown in choice **d.**

107. b. This phrase is written in the passive voice, instead of the active voice. The passive voice is not as direct and clear as the active voice.

108. a. This sentence is best in its original form.

109. b. *To steal* is another example of an irregular verb. The past tense is *stolen* and requires a helping verb in the correct tense to match the subject.

110. c. This sentence contains a double negative. Both *hadn't* and *no* are negatives. Remove one, while maintaining the correct verb tense.

111. d. This sentence is a fragment, missing the main verb. Although several of the choices add a verb, only choice **d** does so without changing the sentence's meaning or making the sentence awkward and confusing.

112. b. This is the most concise version and the one that best expresses the relationship between the clauses. The use of *also* in choice **a** expresses addition when the relationship is really one of simultaneity. Choice **c** has a superfluous comma after *while* and uses a wordy *that* clause. Choice **d** is wordy. Choice **e** makes the original error and uses the vague phrase *find things*.

113. d. This is an example of a comma splice (two independent clauses connected with a comma). To correct this problem, either a semicolon or the right conjunction is needed. Because the conjunctions here do not show the correct relationship between the clauses, adding the semicolon is the best solution.

114. a. This sentence is best in its original form.

115. b. Here, the introductory clause is modifying the meal instead of Melanie. The sentence needs to be rewritten with the modifier in the correct place.

116. a. This sentence is best in its original form.

117. c. This is a question of pronoun use. Because the subject is singular (*winner*), the pronoun must be singular, too. To keep the sentence consistent, it must be *you* to match the other pronoun.

118. a. This sentence is best in its original form.

119. e. The subject of this sentence is *reasons*, which is plural. The verb must agree, so *is* should be *are*.

120. d. The subject in this sentence is compound (*photographs, cards, letters, and other memorabilia*), so the verb has to be plural. Change *fills* to *fill*.

121. c. The pronoun shift needs to be repaired in this sentence. The sentence begins using *you* and then switches to *one*. To stay consistent, the second part of the sentence should also be *you*.

122. b. This is an example of faulty parallelism. The last part of the sentence breaks the pattern and needs to be rewritten with the correct verb tense for consistency.

123. b. This is an error with faulty comparison. The sentence compares one computer to another. Standard usage dictates that you include the word *other.*

124. a. This sentence is best in its original form.

125. c. This is a problem with word choice. The correct term is *formerly,* not *formally.*

126. a. This sentence is best in its original form.

127. a. This sentence is best in its original form. This is another question testing your ability to make the right word choice. *Council* means committee, *counsel* means to give advice, and *consul* means a person appointed to a position by a foreign government.

128. e. This is an example of incorrect word choice. The word that should be used is *breath,* a noun, instead of *breathe,* which is a verb.

129. c. This is a sentence fragment. It is missing the main verb. Only choice **c** provides the main verb in the correct tense.

130. a. This sentence is best in its original form.

131. d. The error in this sentence is the subordinating conjunction in the dependent clause. *Until* does not make sense and does not show the relationship between the ideas. Only the conjunction *unless* corrects this.

132. e. This is an example of a misplaced modifier. As written, the sentence expresses that the chair has been shopping for five hours nonstop, instead of Megan. The modifier has to be moved so that it is modifying the correct noun.

133. c. The subordinating conjunction in this sentence does not make sense. Only the subordinating conjunction *until* makes a logical connection between the ideas.

134. a. This sentence is best in its original form.

135. b. This sentence contains faulty subordination, which makes it difficult to understand. The cause-and-effect relationship between the ideas is lost, and the sentence needs to be rewritten in a logical order.

136. d. Only this answer choice corrects the faulty comparison: Human beings are taller and stronger *than they were* 200 years ago, not taller and stronger *than* 200 years ago. Choice **b** has an apostrophe error in *being's.* Choices **c** and **e** are fragments.

137. b. This is an example of an illogical comparison. As it is written, the sentence states that Carson and science class are both very difficult.

138. a. This sentence is best in its original form.

139. e. This sentence contains a double negative. One of the negatives has to be removed, and the verb tense has to be maintained.

140. d. This is an example of a comma splice, where two independent clauses are connected with a comma. Instead of a comma, the sentence needs a semicolon or an appropriate subordinating conjunction. The conjunctions offered here do not fit, so adding a semicolon is the best solution.

141. b. This is a case of a misplaced modifier. As written, the sentence suggests that the traffic was driving for the first time. The entire sentence needs to be changed so that the introductory clause is modifying the teenager instead of the traffic.

142. e. This question deals with incorrect word choice. The correct word is *elude,* which means to stay just out of reach. *Allude* means to indirectly refer to something.

143. c. This is an example of faulty parallelism. The pattern is adverb and verb, until the last phrase. For consistency, the last phrase needs to be rewritten to match the others.

144. a. This sentence is best in its original form.

145. d. This sentence contains a dependent clause followed by another dependent clause. Removing *so* from the second dependent clause would make it independent.

146. a. This sentence is best in its original form.

147. a. This sentence is best in its original form.

148. b. This is a question about pronoun agreement. Replace the pronoun *your* with *their* to be consistent with the rest of the nouns and pronouns in the sentence.

149. b. This question tests pronoun agreement. The first pronoun is *one*, so *he or she*, not *they*, would maintain consistency.

150. d. This is a sentence fragment. The verb is missing from the second half of the sentence. Only **d** inserts a verb and in the correct tense.

151. e. This is an example of a run-on sentence; it has two independent clauses that are not joined with a conjunction or punctuation. Choice **e** provides the solution by adding a semicolon.

152. b. This is a run-on sentence because it has two independent clauses that are not joined with a conjunction or semicolon. In this answer choice, the appropriate conjunction is added to the introductory clause, making the introductory clause dependent and the sentence grammatically correct.

153. c. This sentence contains a double negative. One of the negatives must be removed to make the sentence correct. In this answer choice, *no* is changed to *any*.

154. d. The main error here is the unclear pronoun reference in *they*, which can refer to either the chemicals or the cancerous cells. Only choice **d** clarifies this by stating *because the chemicals are unable to distinguish*. Choice **a**

is a run-on sentence. Choice **b** is missing a noun or pronoun after *because*. Choices **c** and **e** are illogical.

155. e. This question is looking at pronoun use. In this sentence, a possessive pronoun is needed, so the answer choice with *our* is correct.

156. c. As it is written, this sentence is a fragment, because of the word *that*. By removing *that*, the sentence is corrected.

157. b. This is an example of faulty parallelism. The pattern is interrupted with the last element. In choice **b**, this element is rewritten to make it parallel with rest.

158. d. The modifying clause is in the wrong place in this question. The sentence suggests that the couple is wrapped in a red, satin bow. The clause needs to be moved closer to the noun it modifies, *present*.

159. b. Coordination/subordination, parallel structure, and wordiness are the main issues here. Choice **a** uses the illogical subordinating conjunction *whereas* and lacks parallel structure. Choice **c** uses an incorrect conjunction, is wordy because it uses the passive voice, and is not quite parallel. Choice **d** incorrectly uses *in contrast* instead of expressing addition and uses the passive voice. Choice **e** expresses a logical relationship between the clauses but is wordy and uses the passive voice.

160. a. This sentence is best in its original form.

161. a. This sentence is best in its original form.

Improving Paragraphs Questions

With this type of question, you will be given an example of a student's first draft, which is usually three to five paragraphs long. Multiple questions will be asked about each essay, and these questions may cover a phrase, a few sentences, a whole paragraph, or the entire essay. Each sentence is numbered, so specific sentences are easy to find quickly. You could be asked to revise part of the essay, combine sentences for better flow and organization, or improve content by adding or deleting sentences or pinpointing the main idea.

IMPROVING PARAGRAPHS

1. (a) (b) (c) (d) (e)
2. (a) (b) (c) (d) (e)
3. (a) (b) (c) (d) (e)
4. (a) (b) (c) (d) (e)
5. (a) (b) (c) (d) (e)
6. (a) (b) (c) (d) (e)
7. (a) (b) (c) (d) (e)
8. (a) (b) (c) (d) (e)
9. (a) (b) (c) (d) (e)
10. (a) (b) (c) (d) (e)
11. (a) (b) (c) (d) (e)
12. (a) (b) (c) (d) (e)
13. (a) (b) (c) (d) (e)
14. (a) (b) (c) (d) (e)
15. (a) (b) (c) (d) (e)
16. (a) (b) (c) (d) (e)
17. (a) (b) (c) (d) (e)
18. (a) (b) (c) (d) (e)
19. (a) (b) (c) (d) (e)
20. (a) (b) (c) (d) (e)

21. (a) (b) (c) (d) (e)
22. (a) (b) (c) (d) (e)
23. (a) (b) (c) (d) (e)
24. (a) (b) (c) (d) (e)
25. (a) (b) (c) (d) (e)
26. (a) (b) (c) (d) (e)
27. (a) (b) (c) (d) (e)
28. (a) (b) (c) (d) (e)
29. (a) (b) (c) (d) (e)
30. (a) (b) (c) (d) (e)
31. (a) (b) (c) (d) (e)
32. (a) (b) (c) (d) (e)
33. (a) (b) (c) (d) (e)
34. (a) (b) (c) (d) (e)
35. (a) (b) (c) (d) (e)
36. (a) (b) (c) (d) (e)
37. (a) (b) (c) (d) (e)
38. (a) (b) (c) (d) (e)
39. (a) (b) (c) (d) (e)
40. (a) (b) (c) (d) (e)

41. (a) (b) (c) (d) (e)
42. (a) (b) (c) (d) (e)
43. (a) (b) (c) (d) (e)
44. (a) (b) (c) (d) (e)
45. (a) (b) (c) (d) (e)
46. (a) (b) (c) (d) (e)

▶ Questions

Here are some practice drafts and questions for you to read through. Challenge yourself to see how much you know!

(1) The Chunnel is one of the most remarkable feats of architecture ever created, as it is the underwater tunnel that runs underneath the English Channel between England and France. (2) The incredible notion of connecting those two powerful countries that had been separated for more than 12,000 years had been tossed around for more than two centuries. (3) Everyone from engineers to architects to politicians had come up with a plan or a blueprint. (4) Today, the Chunnel is considered to be one of the true wonders of the modern world for its size and complexity. (5) Also for the fact that it succeeded even though it was full of structural dilemmas. (6) It also had many budget catastrophes and safety nightmares.

(7) The idea for a connection between France and England was first mentioned at the end of the eighteenth century. (8) Although frequently ignored, squashed, and thrown out, the idea just would not die. (9) It continued to pop up again and again for over 200 years. (10) Both European countries were gaining in power and trade between them was on the rise. (11) A century ago, the 20-plus miles that separated them made trade not only slow, but also quite dangerous. (12) Under the best weather conditions, the trip from one coastline to the other took six to eight hours, and frequently, vicious storms delayed ships for days—even weeks. (13) Frustration on both ends grew as shipments fell behind schedule and workers arrived at the docks too seasick to load or unload their cargo. (14) Even later, when ferries and airplanes came along to make the trip faster and safer, passengers still had to put up with paying high transportation fees, standing in crowded airports and other inconveniences.

(15) For decades, the debate had raged over the best way to link these two countries. (16) Ideas ranged from sunken tubes to iron bridges. (17) Which could be easiest and safest—a bridge, a tunnel, or some combination of the two? (18) Every single plan posed some kind of unique problems. (19) A bridge over 20 miles long was a nightmare to try and support. (20) Experts argued that it would cause problems with the many ships that needed to pass through the Channel. (21) Even the best of lighthouses, foghorns, and other precautions not enough to warn a ship that the bridge was ahead. (22) That was asking for a real disaster.

1. Which of the following is the best revision of sentence 1 (reproduced below)?

   The Chunnel is one of the most remarkable feats of architecture ever created, as it is the underwater tunnel which runs underneath the English Channel between England and France.

   a. The Chunnel, one of the most remarkable feats of architecture ever created, is the underwater tunnel which runs underneath the English Channel between England and France.
   b. The Chunnel, or underwater tunnel that runs underneath the English Channel between England and France, is one of the most remarkable feats of architecture ever created.
   c. The underwater tunnel that runs underneath the English Channel between England and France is the Chunnel, which is one of the most remarkable feats of architecture ever created.
   d. Between France and England is the underwater tunnel, which runs underneath the English Channel and is one of the most remarkable feats of architecture ever created, the Chunnel.
   e. The Chunnel, which runs underneath the English Channel between England and France, is an underwater tunnel because it is one of the most remarkable feats of architecture ever created.

2. Which of the following is the best revision of sentence 21 (reproduced below)?

Even the best of lighthouses, foghorns, and other precautions not enough to warn a ship that the bridge was ahead.

    a. Even the best of lighthouses and foghorns and other precautions not enough to warn a ship that the bridge was ahead.

    b. Other precautions, like the best of lighthouses and foghorns, not quite enough to warn a ship that the bridge was ahead.

    c. Even the best of lighthouses, foghorns, and other precautions might not be enough to warn a ship that the bridge was ahead.

    d. Not be quite enough to warn a ship that the bridge was ahead, other precautions, like the best of lighthouses and foghorns.

    e. Even the best of lighthouses, foghorns, and other precautions, just not enough to warn a ship that the bridge was ahead.

3. Which would be the most effective way to combine sentences 4, 5, and 6 (reproduced below)?

Today, the Chunnel is considered to be one of the true wonders of the modern world for its size and complexity. Also for the fact that it succeeded even though it was full of structural dilemmas. It also had many budget catastrophes and safety nightmares.

    a. Today, the Chunnel is considered to be one of the true wonders of the modern world, not only for its size and complexity, but also for the fact that it succeeded even though it was full of structural dilemmas and it had many budget catastrophes and many safety nightmares.

    b. Today, the Chunnel is considered to be one of the true wonders of the modern world for its size and complexity, it succeeded even though it was full of structural dilemmas and it has budget catastrophes and safety nightmares.

    c. Although the Chunnel is considered to be one of the true wonders of the modern world, it is for its size and complexity and for the fact that it succeeded even though it was full of structural dilemmas like budget catastrophes and safety nightmares.

    d. Today, the Chunnel is one of the true wonders of the modern world, not only for its size and complexity, but for the fact that it succeeded even though full of structural dilemmas plus budget catastrophes and also safety nightmares.

    e. Today, the Chunnel is considered to be one of the true wonders of the modern world, not only for its size and complexity, but also for the fact that it succeeded even though it was full of structural dilemmas, budget catastrophes, and safety nightmares.

4. Which of the following best describes the purpose of paragraph 2?

   a. to explain how the Chunnel was originally built

   b. to outline the different construction ideas that were considered

   c. to show the immense complexity of the Chunnel plans

   d. to demonstrate why the Chunnel was truly necessary

   e. to prove that a tunnel was much smarter than a bridge

5. Based on the main idea of paragraph 3, which of the following sentences would be the most effective one to follow sentence 22?

   a. On the other hand, a tunnel built hundreds of feet below the water of the Channel seemed equally risky.

   b. The cost of the project would be truly astronomical and hard to justify to either government.

   c. Prime Minister Margaret Thatcher was especially concerned about getting all of the English and French to use the completed tunnel.

   d. Men from all different professions and backgrounds submitted proposals for every kind of construction possible.

   e. The Chunnel consisted of three tunnels, two running parallel for rail traffic and a third for service and security.

(1) The trapdoor spider cannot spin a web, it must use a different kind of devious strategy in order to capture its desired prey. (2) Instead of spinning a home, it uses its long legs to dig a tunnel in the ground. (3) It's about 11 inches deep. (4) Most of the time, it's two inches wide. (5) It lines the walls with silk, and then, using a combination of silk and dirt, it creates a tricky trapdoor to cover the top. (6) The lid keeps out heat, rain, cold, and predators, plus it fools potential prey.

(7) The trapdoor spider waits for the slightest vibration underneath the hidden door. (8) When it comes along, the spider throws open the door and grabs the unsuspecting prey, from a snack-sized moth or beetle to a feast of a frog or baby bird.

(9) The trapdoor spider's home is not only a hiding place for grabbing meals but also hiding in if the spider feels threatened. (10) These spiders run very quickly and often must escape from intimidating and powerful predators.

6. In context, which word should be placed at the beginning of sentence 1 (reproduced below)?

The trapdoor spider cannot spin a web, it must use a different kind of devious strategy in order to capture its desired prey.

   a. Meanwhile

   b. Because

   c. However

   d. Nonetheless

   e. Fortunately

7. Which of the following is the best way to combine sentences 2, 3, and 4 (reproduced below)?

Instead of spinning a home, it uses its long legs to dig a tunnel in the ground. It's about 11 inches deep. Most of the time, it's two inches wide.

a. Instead of spinning a home, it uses it long lets to dig a tunnel in the ground, it is about 11 inches deep and two inches wide.

b. Instead of spinning a home, they use its long legs to dig a tunnel in the ground and it is about 11 inches deep and about two inches wide.

c. Instead of spinning a home, it uses its long legs to dig a tunnel in the ground about 11 inches deep and two inches wide.

d. Instead of spinning a home, it uses 11 inches deep and two inches wide long legs to dig a tunnel in the ground.

e. Instead of spinning a home, most of the time, it uses its long legs to dig a tunnel in the ground that is 11 inches deep and is just about two inches wide.

8. Which of the following is the best revision for sentence 7 (reproduced below)?

The trapdoor spider waits for the slightest vibration underneath the hidden door.

a. The trapdoor spider wait for the slightest vibration underneath the hidden door.

b. But for the slightest vibration, the trapdoor spider waits underneath the hidden door.

c. The hidden door is where the trapdoor spider wait for the slightest vibration.

d. The trapdoor spider waits underneath the hidden door for the slightest vibration.

e. Although the trapdoor spider waits underneath the hidden door for the slightest vibration.

9. In context, where would the following sentence fit best within the essay?

To do this, they build a few extra hidden entrances, escape tunnels, and side passages for quick getaways.

a. following sentence 1
b. following sentence 4
c. following sentence 7
d. following sentence 9
e. following sentence 10

(1) Curiosity drove Pierre and Marie Curie. (2) Their earlier experiments had found the three minerals that contained the most uranium. (3) However, through a very slow and detailed process, they also discovered something else. (4) There were two other mysterious elements within those minerals in very small quantities. (5) How could they identify them?

(6) It was not a fun or fast procedure. (7) Marie knew that a product called pitchblende was the best to use for their experiments. (8) One sack of it only made a thimbleful of these unknown elements. (9) To get even was a quite a chore.

(10) First the pitchblende was sifted. (11) Then it was ground. (12) Marie boiled it in a big iron pot, stirring for hours with an iron rod. (13) The liquid was thrown away. (14) Pierre would take what was left and treat it with different chemicals. (15) This helped him know which elements he wanted to throw away and which he wanted to study. (16) Between Marie and Pierre, they found them. (17) The first they named polonium in honor of Poland. (18) It is located in eastern Europe. (19) The second one they called radium.

10. Which of the following best describes the purpose of paragraph 3?
  a. to explain the process of separating different minerals
  b. to prove how the Curies discovered uranium
  c. to show how Pierre met and married Marie Curie
  d. to discuss what things can be made with radium
  e. to demonstrate how hard it was to find pitchblende

11. What is the most effective way to combine sentences 10, 11, and 12 (reproduced below)?

First the pitchblende was sifted. Then it was ground. Marie boiled it in a big iron pot, stirring for hours with an iron rod.

  a. First, the pitchblende was sifted, then ground finally boiled in a big iron pot and stirred for hours with an iron rod by Marie.
  b. The pitchblende was first sifted, then ground, and finally boiled in a big iron pot, while Marie stirred it for hours with an iron rod.
  c. First, the pitchblende was sifted, ground by Marie and then it was boiled in a big iron pot, stirring for hours with an iron rod.
  d. Marie, boiled in a big iron pot and stirred for hours with an iron rod, sifted the pitchblende and then ground it.
  e. The big iron pot was stirred for hours with an iron rod by Marie and then the pitchblende was sifted and then ground.

12. Which of the following sentences from the passage should be deleted?
  a. sentence 1
  b. sentence 5
  c. sentence 6
  d. sentence 17
  e. sentence 18

13. In sentence 16, the word *them* could best be replaced with which of the following?
  a. radium
  b. pitchblende
  c. the two elements
  d. polonium
  e. both experiments

(1) A scrapbook is an easy family craft that can reflect the style, format, and contents of its creator's unique personality. (2) All it takes is initiative. (3) Interest and inspiration help too. (4) Begin by choosing a cover style for your scrapbook. (5) You can purchase one premade in a store or create your own. (6) You might want to use a plastic binder with a clear front cover and put stuff on it. (7) Next, choose what theme you want for your scrapbook. (8) Is it for your entire family or just you? (9) Do you want it to focus on school activities alone or your life in general? (10) Perhaps you would like it to just be about spring break or summer vacation.

(11) Do you know what to include in your scrapbook? (12) The more variety you use, the better. (13) How about some photographs, ticket stubs, and postcards? (14) You might want to include personal letters, drawings, report cards, or greeting cards. (15) Other possibilities include newspaper clippings, pressed flowers, concert programs, and certificates. (16) I have all of those in mine and it looks fantastic.

14. Which of the following is the best way to combine sentences 1, 2, and 3 (reproduced below)?

A scrapbook is an easy family craft that can reflect the style, format, and contents of its creator's unique personality. All it takes is initiative. Interest and inspiration help too.

a. A scrapbook is an easy family craft that can reflect the style, format, and contents of its creator's unique personality, all it takes is initiative and interest and inspiration helps too.

b. A scrapbook is an easy family craft that can reflect the style, format, and contents of its creator's unique personality, and all it takes is some initiative, interest, and inspiration.

c. Although a scrapbook is an easy family craft reflecting the style, format, and contents of its creator's unique personality, but it takes initiative, interest, and inspiration.

d. An easy family craft reflecting the style, format, and contents of its creator's unique personality, initiative, interest, and inspiration are need to make a scrapbook.

e. Initiative, interest, and inspiration help the style, format, and contents of the creator's unique personality while making an easy family craft like a scrapbook.

15. Which revision of sentence 6 (reproduced below) is the best?

You might want to use a plastic binder with a clear front cover and put stuff on it.

a. You might want to use a clear binder and then put some stuff on it.

b. Putting some stuff on it, a clear front covered plastic binder could be used.

c. A plastic binder with a clear front cover can be used for all kinds of things.

d. You might want to use a plastic binder with a clear front cover and decorate it.

e. Perhaps you could add a lot of things to the plastic binder's clear front cover.

16. What is the main idea of this essay?

a. what kind of plastic binder you can make for a scrapbook

b. how to arrange photographs and cards in a scrapbook

c. why it is fairly simple for someone to make a scrapbook

d. what themes a person could use for his or her scrapbook

e. when someone should first consider creating a scrapbook

17. Which of the following sentences would fit best following sentence 10?

a. You might even want to add locks of hair, brochures, or magazine articles.

b. You could always make one out of cardboard, construction paper, and glue.

c. The cover should make a statement about who you are and what the theme is.

d. Consider using stickers, glitter, fabric paint, or anything else that you really like.

e. You could also emphasize church activities, school field trips, or your best friends.

18. Which sentence in the essay should be deleted to improve the organization?

a. Begin by choosing a cover style for your scrapbook.

b. Do you want it to focus on school activities alone or your life in general?

c. Do you know what to include in your scrapbook?

d. You might want to include personal letters, drawings, report cards, or greeting cards.

e. I have all of those in mine and it looks fantastic.

(1) One thing about writing well is that it is challenging to do it right, although most teachers will tell you there's really no single correct way to do it, so that's confusing. (2) What I learned in school is that you start with an idea, and some ideas are easier to develop than others. (3) Complicating matters is that sometimes you don't know which one is which until you get into it. (4) Anyway, you start with a first draft, using a technique such as fastwriting. (5) There you take an idea and just start writing about it until you get to the end. (6) The advantage of that is that you don't have to be so critical about what you're writing while you're doing it. (7) You just say what you have to say first and then go back and look over it later and make any changes that you need to. (8) Alternatively, you can start by making an outline. (9) Sometimes, that helps, but sometimes, it makes you less creative, which is a good thing.

(10) Once you get your first draft down, its time to start revising it. (11) You have to look for stuff like run-on sentences, misspelled words, and misplaced modifiers. (12) That's something I do all the time, so now I always watch out for that. (13) And you have to be sure that what you said makes sense. (14) That's the main consideration, and not to be forgotten.

(15) Making your best effort is very important, especially when it comes to writing. (16) Almost everything you do in school, work, or even life, depends on people understanding what you are trying to say. (17) That's why it's vital to be crystal clear in your writing, although that's easier said than done.

19. In the context of the first paragraph, which of the following revisions is best for sentence 1 (reproduced below)?

One thing about writing well is that it is challenging to do it right, although most teachers will tell you there's really no single correct way to do it, so that's confusing.

a. Since most teachers tell you there's no single right way to write well, it can be confusing to try to write right.

b. It's confusing and difficult to write well, although most teachers will tell you there's no single right way to do it.

c. It is difficult to write well, and it's confusing that most teachers say there's no single right way to do it.

d. One thing about writing well that's difficult is that it's confusing for teachers to tell you there's really no single correct way to do it.

e. It's confusing that most teachers tell you there's no single right way to write well, and then it's difficult to do it correctly.

20. Which of the following would be the most clear and concise way to combine sentences 2 and 3 (reproduced below)?

What I learned in school is that you start with an idea, and some ideas are easier to develop than others. Complicating matters is that sometimes you don't know which one is which until you get into it.

a. I learned in school that you start with an idea, but some ideas are easier to develop than others; and, besides, to complicate matters, sometimes you don't know how difficult an idea is until you start writing.

b. In school I learned that you start with an idea, and some ideas are easier to develop than others, but it complicates matters that sometimes you don't know which it is until you get into it.

c. What I learned in school—that you start with an idea—is complicated because some ideas are easier to develop than others, and sometimes you don't know which one is which until you get into it.

d. I learned in school that you start with an idea, but it complicates matters that sometimes you don't know whether or not an idea is easy to develop until you get into it.

e. Although some ideas are easier to develop than others, I learned in school that you start with an idea; and it complicates matters that sometimes you don't know how difficult it is until you get into it.

21. In context, which of the following is the best revision of the underlined portion of sentence 5 (reproduced below)?

There you take an idea and just start writing about it until you get to the end.

a. There an individual

b. As far as fastwriting is concerned, you

c. With this, you

d. There one could

e. In this technique, you

22. Which of the following revisions is most necessary in the final sentence of paragraph 1?
a. No change is necessary.
b. Change the comma to a semicolon.
c. Change *which* to *and creativity*.
d. Change *that* to *an outline*.
e. Change *it* to *an outline*.

(1) More than 500 years ago, a breed of horse was bred for its beauty, strength, and agility. (2) It was known as the Lipizzaner. (3) It was not long before they were made part of the Austrian emperor's royal stables. (4) These elegant and talented horses still exist today, and thousands of people come to watch it perform its amazing tricks.

(5) The first trick the Lipizzaner do are change color. (6) Most of them are born coal-black or brown, but by the time they are ten years old, they have turned white. (7) At the age of three, the most promising young horses are separate from the others and began their training. (8) It is not long before they are paired with a teenage rider who is also in the midst of training. (9) These two will remain together for up to eight years learning skills that require balance and strength on both parts.

(10) By the time they are ready to go on tour for audiences around the world, Lipizzaner can perform pirouettes, powerful kicks, and unbelievable leaps. (11) They enthrall crowds everywhere with their abilities and grace.

23. Which of the following represents the best revision, in context, of the underlined part of sentence 4 (reproduced below)?

These elegant and talented horses still exist today, and thousands of people <u>come to watch it perform its amazing tricks.</u>

a. come to watch him perform his amazing tricks.
b. come to watch them perform their amazing tricks.
c. came to watch it perform its amazing tricks.
d. is coming to watch him perform its amazing tricks.
e. come to watch us perform our amazing tricks.

24. In context, which of the following is the best revision of sentence 5 (reproduced below)?

The first trick the Lipizzaner do are change color.

a. The first trick the Lipizanner's do are change color.
b. The first trick the Lipizzaner does is change color.
c. The first trick the Lipizzaner's did is change color.
d. The first trick the Lipizzaner do is change color.
e. The first trick the Lipizanners are doing is change color.

25. In context, which of the following is the best revision of sentence 7 (reproduced below)?

At the age of three, the most promising young horses are separate from the others and began their training.

a. At the age of three, the most promising young horses, although separate from the others, began their training.
b. At the age of three, the most promising young horses are separating from the others and beginning their training.
c. At the age of three, the most promising young horses separate and began training from the others.
d. At the age of three, the most promising young horses are separated from the others and beginning their training.
e. At the age of three, the most promising young horses are separated from the others and begin their training.

26. What is the main purpose of the essay's second paragraph?
a. to outline the training that the Lipizzaner go through in life
b. to provide background on where the Lipizzaner horses first came from
c. to show all of the different tricks these horses learn how to perform
d. to describe a Lipizzaner performance to potential future audiences
e. to demonstrate the extensive history of the Lipizzaner breeding line

27. The logical flow of the passage as a whole would be most improved by making which of the following changes to the second paragraph?

   a. After sentence 5, insert a sentence listing the other tricks the horses can do.

   b. After sentence 6, insert a sentence naming the scientific process of how their color changes.

   c. After sentence 7, insert a sentence about how the horses respond to separation.

   d. After sentence 8, insert a sentence detailing which teenagers are chosen.

   e. After sentence 9, insert a sentence describing the exercises they do together.

(1) Do you want to spice up your school days? Would you like the other kids in school to know more about you without ever saying a word? (2) Why not decorate your locker?

(3) School lockers can be quite dull on the outside. (4) Each one looks just like the one on either side of it. (5) There isn't much you can do about that putting things on the outside of your locker is usually frowned upon in most public school systems. (6) The inside, however, is your own personal space and one can decorate it in many unique ways to reflect their distinct individuality.

(7) Fortunately, in recent years, a number of companies have manufactured various kinds of locker gear. (8) You can go to most large department stores and find mirrors, shelves, photo frames or pen and pencil holders. (9) Beyond what you can buy, however, you can also create on your own.

(10) For example, you can take some of your favorite toys or figurines. (11) Add peel and stick magnets to the back of them. (12) You can also laminate your drawings and turn them into magnets as well. (13) This way, you can stick them on the sides, top or bottom of your locker. (14) Be sure to avoid using tape or any kind of glue. (15) You want to be able to remove your things at the end of the school year!

28. In context, which of the following is the best revision of sentence 5 (reproduced below)?

   There isn't much you can do about that putting things on the outside of your locker is usually frowned upon in most public school systems.

   a. There isn't much you can do about that so putting things on the outside of your locker is usually frowned upon in most public school systems.

   b. There isn't much you can do about that because putting things on the outside of your locker is usually frowned upon in most public school systems.

   c. There isn't much you can do about that, putting things on the outside of your locker is usually frowned upon in most public school systems.

   d. There isn't much you can do about putting things on the outside of your locker is usually frowned upon in most public school systems.

   e. There isn't much you can do about that, however, putting things on the outside of your locker is usually frowned upon in most public school systems.

29. In context, which of the following represents the best way to revise and combine sentences 10, 11, and 12 (reproduced below)?

For example, you can take some of your favorite toys or figurines. Add peel and stick magnets to the back of them. You can also laminate your drawings and turn them into magnets as well.

a. For example, take some of your favorite toys or figurines or laminate some of your drawings and then add peel and stick magnets to the back of them to turn them all into magnets.

b. Take some of your favorite toys or figurines, plus your laminated drawings, for example, and add peel and stick magnets to the back of them to turn them into magnets as well.

c. For example, you can take some of your favorite toys or figurines or laminated drawings and add peel and stick magnets to the back of them.

d. By adding peel and stick magnets to the back of your favorite toys or figurines or some of your laminated drawings, you can turn them all into magnets.

e. Laminate your favorite drawings and then put peel and stick magnets on the back of them or take some of your toys and figurines and do the same thing to them.

30. Which of the following sentences, if added after sentence 9, would best serve to link the third paragraph to the fourth paragraph?
a. You can often do this just by using typical items already found in your home.
b. The typical school locker is gray, metal, and features nothing more than a number.
c. Many sites found on the Internet feature a huge variety of locker products for sale.
d. You can let people glimpse into what is important to you by doing this.
e. If you don't, you will most likely be hearing from your school administration.

31. Which of the following represents the best revision, in context, of the underlined part of sentence 6 (reproduced below)?

The inside, however, is your own personal space and <u>one can decorate it in many unique ways to reflect their distinct individuality.</u>

a. one can decorate it in many unique ways to reflect one's distinct personality.
b. they can decorate it in many unique ways to reflect their distinct personality.
c. he can decorate it in many unique ways to reflect his distinct personality.
d. you can decorate it in many unique ways to reflect your distinct personality.
e. we can decorate it in many unique ways to reflect our distinct personality.

(1) Most 18-year-olds spend their time getting ready for graduation. (2) Some are preparing for college. (3) Others are looking for full-time jobs. (4) A young man named Michael Sessions has far different plans. (5) He is working on an outline for what he wants to achieve as one of the country's youngest mayors in history.

(6) In the November 2005 elections held in Hillsdale, Michigan, Sessions, a high school senior, received over 700 votes and found himself the new major of his small town. (7) He ran his entire campaign off the $700 that he earned during the summer. (8) He used it to go door to door throughout his city, meeting people. (9) The personal touch was quite successful. (10) Sessions was too young to sign up at the time of the spring registration for candidates, so he waited until he turned 18 and then entered as a write-in candidate. (11) This meant that voters had to remember it and write it on the ballot in order to vote for him.

(12) Although Sessions is still in school, he performs his mayoral duties in the late afternoons, evenings, and weekends. (13) He plans to keep this schedule up when he attends college in the autumn.

32. In context, which of the following represents the best way to revise and combine sentences 1, 2, and 3 (reproduced below)?

Most 18-year-olds spend their time getting ready for graduation. Some are preparing for college. Others are looking for full-time jobs.

a. Most 18-year-olds spend their time getting ready for graduation, preparing for college, or looking for full-time jobs.

b. Most 18-year-olds spend their time getting ready for graduation, prepare for college or look for full-time jobs.

c. Most 18-year-olds spending their time getting ready for graduation, preparing for college, or looking for full-time jobs.

d. Most 18-year-olds spend their time get ready for graduation, prepare for college, and look for full-time jobs.

e. Most 18-year-olds spend their time getting ready for graduation, preparing for college, and looked for full-time jobs.

33. In the context of the passage as a whole, which of the following is the best way to revise the underlined portion of sentence 11 (reproduced below)?

This meant that voters had to remember it and write it on the ballot in order to vote for him.

a. This meant that they had to remember it and write

b. This meant that voters had to remember his name and write

c. This meant that voters have been remembering it and write

d. This meant that voters had to remember it and wrote

e. This meant that voters remembered it and wrote

34. What is the main idea of this passage as a whole?

a. how to get elected to a political office while still in high school

b. what life is like the small city of Hillsdale, Michigan

c. how a high school student got elected to office

d. why Sessions was able to beat out the area incumbent

e. where to get a summer job in order to pay for a campaign

35. In context, which word should be placed at the beginning of sentence 4 (reproduced below)?

A young man named Michael Sessions has far different plans.

a. Unfortunately

b. Because

c. Unknowingly

d. However

e. Clearly

(1) The vast majority of schools entered the high-tech age years ago by installing computers throughout their libraries. (2) They also placed them in their classrooms. (3) All administrative offices were equipped with computer systems as well. (4) The new trend, however, is taking this one step further at an innovative school in Arizona, which is providing an all new way for students to do their homework. (5) They provide them with their own laptop!

(6) Instead of using money to buy all new textbooks for Empire High School, laptop computers were bought by the administration with the funds. (7) The teachers commonly select educational materials on the Internet for students to consult to complete homework assignments. (8) To make the laptops feel more personal, students are allowed to store their own music collections on them.

(9) Instead of handing in reports and homework on paper, these Arizona students just e-mail it into their individual teachers. (10) So much for that old excuse that the dog ate your homework!

36. In context, which of the following is the best way to revise sentence 5 (reproduced below)?

They provide them with their own laptop!

a. They provide the student with their own laptops!
b. The school provides them with their own laptops!
c. The students provide them with our own laptops!
d. The school provides the students with the own laptop!
e. The school provides each of the students with his or her own laptop!

37. In context, which of the following is the best way to revise sentence 6 (reproduced below)?

Instead of using money to buy all new textbooks for Empire High School, laptop computers were bought by the administration with the funds.

a. Instead of using money to buy all new textbooks for Empire High School, the funds were used by the administration to buy laptop computers.
b. Instead of using money to buy all new textbooks, laptop computers were bought with the money by the administration for Empire High School.
c. Laptop computers were bought by the administration with the funds that were supposed to go to buy all new textbooks for Empire High School.
d. Instead of using money to buy all new textbooks for Empire High School, the administration used the funds to purchase laptop computers.
e. Empire High School administration took the money for buying all new textbooks and instead they used it to buy laptop computers.

38. In context, which of the following represents the best way to revise and combine sentences 1, 2, and 3 (reproduced below)?

The vast majority of schools entered the high-tech age years ago by installing computers throughout their libraries. They also placed them in their classrooms. All administrative offices were equipped with computer systems as well.

a. The vast majority of schools entered the high-tech age years ago by installing computers throughout their libraries and in their classrooms and lastly, in their administrative offices as well.
b. The vast majority of schools entered the high-tech age years ago by installing computers throughout their libraries and classrooms and they equipped all of the administrative offices too.
c. The vast majority of schools entered the high-tech age years ago by installing computers throughout their libraries, classrooms, and administrative offices.
d. The vast majority of schools entered the high-tech age by installing computers in libraries, classrooms, and offices for the administration.
e. The vast majority of schools entered the high-tech age years ago by installing, throughout their libraries, classrooms and administrative offices, computers.

39. Which of the following best describes the purpose of the first paragraph?

   a. to explain how the students do their homework on computers

   b. to point out how schools have entered the computer age

   c. to demonstrate where the money for the computers came from

   d. to show how the students make the computers their own

   e. to discuss how teachers use online sites for homework help

40. This passage discusses everything EXCEPT

   a. the different ways students can carry their laptops.

   b. the role of computers in modern high schools.

   c. the ways teachers can utilize websites for teaching.

   d. the new method of e-mailing in homework assignments.

   e. the innovative teaching methods at Empire High School.

(1) In a day and age where storytelling is beginning to be considered one of the lost arts and keeping records means booting up instead of write down, families may find themselves wondering how to create and preserving their genealogy. (2) Perhaps they want to just save the family stories or trace the most recent generations. (3) Others might want to explore their families' role in history or just put something together to commemorate an anniversary or other important event. (4) Putting together a family tree may sound like a great idea, but how do you even begin to make the first step, and how can it be a total family project?

(5) Investigating the many different people who came before you is a multilayered task that involves asking questions and doing research. (6) It also takes combing through real and virtual archives. (7) Perhaps even a field trip or two to places like cemeteries. (8) After all, a graveyard is really like a museum without walls since it contains fascinating historical artifacts that are hundreds of years old, all in the form of gravestones. (9) Cemeteries are not the scary places that many horror films try to convey.

(10) Another great source are the census records that can be found on the Internet. (11) Often, you find out more than just birth and death records. (12) Resources for information include National Archives, as well as local family records. (13) Your local library can connect you with basic genealogy guidebooks and reference books as well.

(14) Make sure not to overlook one of the best resources of all—your family. (15) Grandparents, uncles, aunts, and cousins are often wonderful sources of stories, traditions, facts, and other helpful information. (16) Taking the time to talk to them about this can bring all of you closer—another side benefit from a project like this one.

41. Which is the best revision of sentence 10 (reproduced below)?

Another great source are the census records that can be found on the Internet.

   a. Another great source is the census records that can be found on the Internet.

   b. Another great source was the census records that can be found on the Internet.

   c. Another great source are the census records that will be found on the Internet.

   d. Another great source is the census records that are be found on the Internet.

   e. Another great sources were the census records that can be found on the Internet.

42. Which of the following is the best revision of sentence 1 (reproduced below)?

In a day and age where storytelling is beginning to be considered one of the lost arts and keeping records means booting up instead of write down, families may find themselves wondering how to create and preserving their genealogy.

a. In a day and age where storytelling is beginning to be considered one of the lost arts and keeping records means boot up instead of write down, families may find themselves wondering how to create and preserve their genealogy.

b. In a day and age where storytelling is beginning to be considered one of the lost arts and keep records means booting up instead of writing down, families may find themselves wonderful how to creating and preserving their genealogy.

c. In a day and age where storytelling is beginning to be considered one of the lost arts and keeping records means booting up instead of writing down, families may find themselves wondering how to create and preserve their genealogy.

d. In a day and age where storytelling is beginning to be considered one of the lost arts and kept records means boot up instead of write down, families may found themselves wondering how to create and preserve their genealogy.

e. In a day and age where storytelling began to be considered one of the lost arts and keeping records means booting up instead of writing down, families may find themselves wondering how to create and preserve their genealogy.

43. Which is the best way to combine sentences 5, 6, and 7 (reproduced below)?

Investigating the many different people who came before you is a multilayered task that involves asking questions and doing research. It also takes combing through real and virtual archives. Perhaps even a field trip or two to places like cemeteries.

a. Investigating the many different people who came before you is a multilayered task that involves asking questions, doing research, combing through real and virtual archives, and a field trip or two to places like cemeteries.

b. Investigating the many different people who came before you is a multilayered task that involves asking questions, doing research, combing through real and virtual archives, and even taking a field trip or two to places like cemeteries.

c. Investigating the many different people who came before you is a multilayered task that is involving asking questions, doing research, combing through real and virtual archives, and even taking a field trip or two to places like cemeteries.

d. Investigating the many different people who came before you is a multilayered task that involves ask questions, do research, comb through real and virtual archives, and take a field trip or two to places like cemeteries.

e. Investigate the many different people who came before you is a multilayered task that involves asking questions, doing research, combing through real and virtual archives and taking a field trip or two to places like cemeteries.

44. To improve the coherence of paragraph 2, which of the following sentences would be the best to delete?
a. sentence 4
b. sentence 7
c. sentence 9
d. sentence 12
e. sentence 14

45. Which of the following sentences is most in need of further support and development?
a. Others might want to explore their families' role in history or just put something together to commemorate an anniversary or other important event.
b. Your local library can connect you with basic genealogy guidebooks and reference books as well.
c. Make sure not to overlook one of the best resources of all—your family.
d. Often, you find out more than just birth and death records.
e. Taking the time to talk to them about this can bring all of you closer—another side benefit from a project like this one.

46. Which of the following is the best revision of sentence 16 (reproduced below)?

Taking the time to talk to them about this can bring all of you closer—another side benefit from a project like this one.

a. Taking the time to talk to them about this can bring all of them closer—another side benefit from a project like this one.
b. Taking the time to talk to them about family stories can bring all of you closer—another side benefit from a project like this one.
c. Taking the time to talk to us about family stories can bring us all closer—another side benefit from a project like this one.
d. Taking the time to talk to you about this can bring all of you closer—another side benefit from a project like this one.
e. Taking the time to talk to everyone about stuff can bring all of you closer—another side benefit from a project like this one.

▶ Answers

1. b. This is a revision question. It takes one of the awkward sentences from the essay and asks you to figure out how to correct any mistakes in it. In this sentence, the description of the Chunnel is at the end of the sentence instead of next to what it is describing. Choices **a**, **c**, **d**, and **e** are all wordy and awkward. Only choice **b** eliminates extra words and moves the descriptive phrase where it belongs.

2. c. This sentence fragment is missing the necessary verb. The other choices move the words around but do not provide the required verb to form a complete sentence.

3. e. This is a sentence combining question. Your job is to figure out the best way to combine three sentences into one in order to more accurately express the sentence's meaning. Choices **a** and **d** are wordy; choice **b** is a run-on sentence; and choice **c** makes no sense. Only choice **e** retains all necessary information in a more efficient manner.

4. d. This is a content question. It is asking about a section of the essay; in this case, the question asks about the second paragraph. You need to figure out what the main idea of the second paragraph is. Choices **a**, **b**, and **c** are main ideas of the first paragraph, and choice **e** is the main idea of the last paragraph.

5. a. You are being asked how to tie the information together. Choice **b** deals with cost, which is covered in another section of the essay. Choice **c** is irrelevant to the information covered in the essay. Choice **d** belongs earlier in the essay. Choice **e** is truthful information but not relevant to the essay.

6. b. The dependent clause at the beginning of this sentence needs an introductory word to make it complete, but the word has to show the relationship between the clause and the rest of the sentence. *Meanwhile* implies a time relationship, which does not apply. *However* and *nonetheless* imply contrast, which also does not apply. *Fortunately* implies good news, and does not work for this sentence. Only *because* fits; this word explains why a different strategy is needed.

7. c. This question requires you to put together three sentences into one grammatically correct sentence without losing the original meanings. Choice **a** is a run-on sentence. Choice **b** uses the wrong pronouns. Choice **d** does not make sense, and choice **e** is wordy and contains unnecessary information.

8. d. This is a case of a misplaced modifier. The phrase *underneath the hidden door* is describing where the spider is hiding, not the vibration. Choice **a** does not repair this, choice **b** makes no sense, choice **c** has the wrong verb tense, and choice **e** is a sentence fragment.

9. e. This is a content question, and you have to decide where the information best fits into the essay overall. This information better fits at the end of the essay, following sentence 10.

10. a. This content question singles out a specific paragraph and asks you to figure out its main idea. In this case, the paragraph focused on a very detailed and specific process of separating different materials, not on how the Curies

met, how they discovered uranium, what can be made with radium, or how to find pitchblende.

11. b. This question is tricky; you have a lot of information to put together and in a logical order. Only choice **b** does this correctly.

12. e. This content question asks you to remove the unnecessary sentence. Choices **a**, **b**, **c**, and **d** are all relevant to each other. Choice **e**, however, contains unnecessary extra information.

13. c. This is a pronoun reference problem. *Them* refers to two nouns from the previous sentence.

14. b. Choice **a** is a run-on sentence. Choice **c** has a dependent clause introduced by *although*, which does not fit with the coordinating conjunction *but*. Choice **d** has a problem with wordiness and verb tense, and choice **e** is confusing and loses the sentence's original meaning.

15. d. The biggest problem in this statement is the word *stuff*. It is a poor word choice because it is too general. Choices **a** and **b** don't change this word. Choices **c** and **e** change the meaning of the original sentence. By replacing *stuff* with *decorate*, the sentence is much more precise.

16. c. Here, you need to pinpoint the main point of the entire essay. Although choices **a**, **b**, **d**, and **e** were all in the essay, they were supporting details instead of the main point.

17. e. To answer this, you have to go back and reread sentence 10 to identify the subject. In this case, the subject is what kind of theme you want for your scrapbook.

18. e. Once again, you are identifying which sentence must be deleted. The one that clearly does not belong is choice **e** because it shifts from *you* to *I*.

19. c. The sentence, as written, is confusing. There are several pronouns without clear antecedents, which must be clarified. Choice **b** misplaces the confusion caused by teachers. Choices **a** and **d** are unnecessarily wordy, as is choice **e**. Only choice **c** expresses the author's intention clearly and concisely.

20. d. These two sentences have three essential ideas, all of which need to be conveyed clearly and concisely. The phrase in the second sentence *until you get into it* is problematic, in that there's no clear antecedent to *it*. Choices **b** and **c** repeat this ambiguity. Choice **d** clearly makes *idea* the antecedent of *it*. Choice **e** is unnecessarily wordy and also fails to clearly establish the antecedent of *it*.

21. e. The problem with the underlined portion of the sentence is that *there* is vague, with an unclear antecedent. By calling fastwriting a *technique*, you clarify the concept as well as the sentence. Choice **b** is needlessly wordy and repetitive. Choices **a** and **c** does not correct the unclear reference problem, nor does choice **d**, which also suffers from stuffy hypercorrectness that doesn't mesh with the overall tone.

22. c. The primary problem with this sentence is that the antecedent of *which* is unclear. As written, the sentence makes creativity sound like an undesirable quality in writing. The word *but*, however, makes it clear that this is not the author's intention. None of the other answer choices addresses this problem.

23. b. The error here is the pronoun in the underlined part of the sentence. The noun is *horses*, which is plural, but the pronoun used is singular. The pronoun should be changed to *their*.

24. d. If the noun was *Lipizanner*, you would need the plural verb *are*. However, the noun is *trick*, which is singular, so you need the verb *is*.

25. e. This sentence contains verb tense problems. The only choice that gets both verb forms correct is choice **e**.

26. a. This content question asks you to identify the main idea of the essay's second paragraph. The essay does provide background, but in another paragraph. The different tricks are not listed, and a performance is mentioned but not described. Brief history is

given, but not extensive history. The correct answer is choice **a**.

27. e. This is another type of content question where it would be best to insert some additional information. In choices **a**, **b**, **c**, and **d**, the suggested extra information is unnecessary and not related to the rest of the essay strongly enough.

28. b. This is a run-on sentence, because it is two complete sentences put together without proper punctuation or conjunctions. The conjunction *so* does not work in the sentence, as in choice **a**. Choice **c** only adds a comma, so it is still a run-on sentence. Choice **d** is still a run-on sentence. Choice **e**, which adds *however*, implies a contrast and does not fit with the rest of the sentence.

29. c. This question is asking you to combine three sentences into one. It is easy to become too wordy as in choices **a**, **b**, **d**, and **e**. Only choice **c** takes out unnecessary words and retains the sentence's original meaning.

30. a. This content question is asking you to improve the coherence and organization of the essay by adding another sentence to move from one paragraph to the next. To make sure you have made the correct choice, you have to reread the sentences around it. The only one of the five choices that relates to the topic of finding things to decorate your locker with is choice **a**.

31. d. In this revision question, the problem is the pronoun. The essay has been using the pronoun *you* and suddenly switches to *one* and the pronoun *their*. Only choice **d** corrects both pronouns to keep them in line with the rest of the essay.

32. a. The key to combining these three sentences is keeping the verbs parallel throughout, as in choice **a**. The verbs all need to end in *-ing*.

33. b. This is an example of a vague pronoun that impedes meaning. The pronoun *it* needs to be replaced with the words *his name*.

34. c. You need to have an idea of what this entire essay is about to answer this question correctly. It is not an essay on how to get elected or what life is like in Hillsdale. It does not list the ways Sessions beat the incumbent. Although a summer job is mentioned, it is not mentioned in detail to show how he financed the campaign.

35. d. You need to reread the sentences, so you understand the relationship among them. The only answer choice that shows that relationship correctly uses *however* to show contrast.

36. e. The problem in this sentence is an indefinite pronoun. The combination of *they*, *them*, and *their* in the sentence is confusing. Only choice **e** replaces the pronouns to make the sentence more understandable.

37. d. The introductory clause in this sentence is about the administration, not about the computers. Choice **a** does not repair this; it just repeats the problem by putting the word *funds* where the word *computers* was. Choice **b** also repeats the original problem. Choice **c** is confusing, and choice **e** is awkward.

38. c. There are a lot of extra words in these three sentences and most of these words need to be eliminated in order to make the sentence read smoothly and clearly.

39. b. Here, you have to figure out the overall message of the first paragraph. All the other choices are about topics that are found in other sections of the essay.

40. a. This question is testing you to see if you can pinpoint the one topic that is not covered anywhere in the essay. In this case, the only one that is not mentioned is choice **a**.

41. a. The problem with this sentence is subject-verb agreement. It is easy to think that the subject is *records*, which is plural, but the subject of the sentence is really *source*, which is singular.

42. c. There are a lot of verb tenses in this statement. You have to carefully choose the choice that maintains the correct verb tense throughout the sentence.

43. b. You have to make sure all the verbs are the same tense and parallel throughout this sentence.

44. c. This content question asks you to pick the sentence that does not belong in the essay. The only sentence that veers off topic is about cemeteries in scary movies. The rest of the choices are all relevant and relate directly to the main idea.

45. d. Here, you need to find out what statement in the essay is not expanded on enough; it is lacking in specifics and the essay would be stronger by adding more details. In this case, the best solution is choice **d**. Although this choice mentions finding more than just birth and death records, it stops there. It does not say what else you might find.

46. b. This is a case of an indefinite pronoun. Choice **b** is the only answer choice that clarifies the pronouns to make the sentence understandable.

5 ▶ Responding to Quotation Prompts

When you take the essay portion of the SAT, you should construct a strong point of view, convey your ideas in coherent order, and implement accurate language.

You will be required to write your essay on the lines provided on your answer sheet, and no additional paper will be distributed. To ensure that you have enough space for your essay, do not use wide margins and keep your handwriting to a reasonable size. Remember to write legibly for the trained high school and college teachers who will be scoring your essay.

When answering the practice writing prompts in this chapter, give yourself about 25 minutes, which is how much time you will have during the actual SAT. Be careful not to write on another topic when answering these prompts; during the SAT, an off-topic essay will be given a score of zero.

1. *"Creativity is allowing oneself to make mistakes. Art is knowing which ones to keep."* —Scott Adams

Assignment: What is your opinion on the relationship between mistakes and creativity? Plan your response and support your position with specific points and examples from your observations, studies, reading, or personal experiences.

2. *"Even if smog were a risk to human life, we must remember that life in nature, without technology, is wholesale death."* —Ayn Rand

"If it keeps up, man will atrophy all his limbs but the push-button finger." —Frank Lloyd Wright

Assignment: Consider the two contrasting statements. Choose the quotation that most closely reflects your viewpoint. Write an essay that explains your choice. Plan your response and support your position with specific points and examples from your observations, studies, reading, or personal experiences.

3. *"I didn't belong as a kid and that always bothered me. If only I'd known that one day my differentness would be an asset, then my early life would have been much easier."* —Bette Midler

Assignment: How do you view things that are different around you in your life? Plan your response and support your position with specific points and examples from your observations, studies, reading, or personal experiences.

4. *"If you have made mistakes . . . there is always another chance for you . . . you may have a fresh start any moment you choose, for this thing we call 'failure' is not the falling down, but the staying down."* —Mary Pickford

Assignment: How can a person use failure to improve his or her life? Plan your response and support your position with specific points and examples from your observations, studies, reading, or personal experiences.

5. *"Until you have learned to be tolerant with those who do not always agree with you; until you have cultivated the habit of saying some kind word of those whom you do not admire; until you have formed the habit of looking for the good instead of the bad there is in others, you will be neither successful nor happy."* —Napoleon Hill

Assignment: Are these the elements you need to be able to achieve happiness and success? Plan your response and support your position with specific points and examples from your observations, studies, reading, or personal experiences.

6. *In one of his most famous lines, Shakespeare's Hamlet says, "I must be cruel, only to be kind."*

Assignment: Do situations exist where an individual must be cruel in order to be kind? Plan your response and support your position with specific points and examples from your observations, studies, reading, or personal experiences.

7. *"You can make more friends in two months by becoming interested in other people than you can in two years by trying to get other people interested in you."* —Dale Carnegie

> **Assignment:** Is Carnegie's idea the best way to make friends? Plan your response and support your position with specific points and examples from your observations, studies, reading, or personal experiences.

8. *"I know you've heard it a thousand times before. But it's true—hard work pays off. If you want to be good, you have to practice, practice, practice. If you don't love something, then don't do it."* —Ray Bradbury

> **Assignment:** Is it possible in today's society to only spend your time doing something you enjoy? Plan your response and support your position with specific points and examples from your observations, studies, reading, or personal experiences.

9. *"How far you go in life depends on your being tender with the young, compassionate with the aged, sympathetic with the striving, and tolerant of the weak and the strong. Because someday in life you will have been all of these."* —George Washington Carver

> **Assignment:** How can relating to someone cause you to go far in life? Plan your response and support your position with specific points and examples from your observations, studies, reading, or personal experiences.

10. *"The worst sin towards our fellow creatures is not to hate them, but to be indifferent to them; that's the essence of inhumanity."* —George Bernhard Shaw

> **Assignment:** Can being indifferent toward others affect them in negative ways? Plan your response and support your position with specific points and examples from your observations, studies, reading, or personal experiences.

11. *"To be nobody but yourself—in a world which is doing its best, night and day, to make you everybody else—means to fight the hardest battle which any human being can fight; and never stop fighting."* —E.E. Cummings

> **Assignment:** Is being yourself a challenge in today's world? Plan your response and support your position with specific points and examples from your observations, studies, reading, or personal experiences.

12. *"There are three kinds of death in this world. There's heart death, there's brain death, and there's being off the network."* —Guy Almes

> *"I'd wipe the machines off the face of the earth again, and end the industrial epoch absolutely, like a black mistake."* —D.H. Lawrence

> **Assignment:** Consider the two contrasting statements. Choose the quotation that most closely reflects your viewpoint. Write an essay that explains your choice. Plan your response and support your position with specific points and examples from your observations, studies, reading, or personal experiences.

13. Thomas Edison, the renowned inventor, is famous for having said, "Genius is one percent inspiration, ninety-nine percent perspiration."

Assignment: Do you agree with this definition of genius? Plan your response and support your position with specific points and examples from your observations, studies, reading, or personal experiences.

14. *"Aerodynamically, the bumble bee shouldn't be able to fly, but the bumble bee doesn't know it, so it goes on flying anyway."* —Mary Kay Ash

Assignment: What does this imply about the bee? How does this information then apply to people in general? Plan your response and support your position with specific points and examples from your observations, studies, reading, or personal experiences.

15. *"Courage is not the absence of fear but the mastery of it."* —Mark Twain

"Feel the fear—and do it anyway." —Susan Jeffers

Assignment: Consider the two contrasting statements. Choose the quotation that most closely reflects your viewpoint. Write an essay that explains your choice. Plan your response and support your position with specific points and examples from your observations, studies, reading, or personal experiences.

16. *"I like nonsense; it wakes up the brain cells. Fantasy is a necessary ingredient in living; it's a way of looking at life through the wrong end of a telescope. Which is what I do, and that enables you to laugh at life's realities."* —Dr. Suess

Assignment: Are fantasy and nonsense necessary elements in daily life? Plan your response and support your position with specific points and examples from your observations, studies, reading, or personal experiences.

17. *"Are you bored with life? Then throw yourself into some work you believe in with all your heart, live for it, die for it, and you will find happiness that you had thought could never be yours."* —Dale Carnegie

Assignment: Do you agree or disagree that this is the best solution to boredom? Plan your response and support your position with specific points and examples from your observations, studies, reading, or personal experiences.

18. *"People are always blaming their circumstances for what they are. I do not believe in circumstances. The people who get on in this world are the people who get up and look for the circumstances they want, and if they cannot find them, make them."* —George Bernard Shaw

Assignment: Can people create their own personal circumstances or are they at the mercy of those circumstances? Plan your response and support your position with specific points and examples from your observations, studies, reading, or personal experiences.

19. Alexander Smith said, "The great man is the man who does a thing for the first time."

> **Assignment:** Do you agree with this definition of greatness? Plan your response and support your position with specific points and examples from your observations, studies, reading, or personal experiences.

20. The inventor and statesman Benjamin Franklin said, "Money never made a man happy yet, nor will it. There is nothing in its nature to produce happiness."

> **Assignment:** Can money produce happiness? Plan your response and support your position with specific points and examples from your observations, studies, reading, or personal experiences.

▶ Scoring Guide and Sample Essays

As the expert graders score your paper, they will be grading it holistically. This means that rather than using a point system that awards you a certain number of points for each component, they will be looking at your response as a whole and awarding it a score. However, as they determine that overall score, the graders will be focusing on four areas: meaning (content), development (support), organization (flow of ideas), and language use or mechanics (grammar).

Although a specific point value is not assigned for each component, these are the areas that will be assessed and considered when the grader arrives at a score. Scores range from a low of 1 (showing writing incompetence) to a maximum of 6 (demonstrating clear and consistent competence). The graders will focus on the strength of your argument. In addition to looking for this content, the graders will be paying attention to your writing style.

A modified copy of the grading guidelines follows:

6 points

- Demonstrates outstanding writing skills
- Includes a clear and insightful point of view and reflects excellent critical thinking, using strong examples and other evidence to support the point of view
- Contains strong organization and focus, a sense of unity, and a skillful flow of ideas
- Demonstrates a strong command of language, with varied and appropriate word choice and meaningful variation in sentence structure
- Contains few, if any, errors in grammar, usage, and mechanics

5 points

- Demonstrates effective writing skills
- Includes a clear point of view and reflects strong critical thinking, using effective examples and other evidence to support the point of view
- Contains strong organization and focus, a sense of unity, and a flow of ideas
- Demonstrates a good command of language, with appropriate word choice and variation in sentence structure
- Contains few errors in grammar, usage, and mechanics

4 points

- Demonstrates competent writing skills, but the quality of the writing may be inconsistent
- Includes a point of view and reflects competent critical thinking, using sufficient examples to support the point of view
- Contains a general organizational plan and focus, with some unity and flow of ideas
- Demonstrates a sufficient but inconsistent command of language, with mostly appropriate word choice and some variation in sentence structure
- Contains some errors in grammar, usage, and mechanics

3 points

- Demonstrates inadequate but not incompetent writing skills
- Includes a point of view that reflects some critical thinking, but the point of view may be inconsistent or incomplete, and support may be lacking
- Contains a limited organizational strategy and focus, with a weak or inconsistent sense of unity and flow of ideas
- Demonstrates a developing but weak command of language, with weak or inappropriate vocabulary, little or no variation in sentence structure, and may contain errors in sentence construction
- Contains many errors in grammar, usage, and mechanics

2 points

- Demonstrates limited writing skills and may contain serious flaws
- Includes a limited or vague point of view and reflects poor critical thinking, using inadequate or irrelevant examples or other support
- Displays a weak sense of organization and/or focus, and may lack unity and/or flow of ideas
- Demonstrates an inadequate command of language, with limited or incorrect vocabulary, and incorrect or flawed sentence structure
- Contains serious errors in grammar, usage, and/or mechanics that may make the writing difficult to understand

1 point

- Demonstrates incompetence in writing and contains serious flaws
- Does not contain a point of view, or provides little or no support for the point of view
- Lacks organization and/or focus, unity, and a flow of ideas
- Contains serious errors in vocabulary and sentence structure
- Contains serious errors in grammar, usage, and/or mechanics that make the writing difficult to understand

0 points

- An essay that does not address the prompt or is blank receives a zero.

(Adapted from The College Board)

Sample Essays

3. *"I didn't belong as a kid and that always bothered me. If only I'd known that one day my differentness would be an asset, then my early life would have been much easier."* —Bette Midler

> **Assignment:** How do you view things that are different around you in your life? Plan your response and support your position with specific points and examples from your observations, studies, reading, or personal experiences.

Score 6 Essay

More than 50 years ago, psychologist Abraham Maslow created what he called a hierarchy of needs. It was a pyramid representation of what human beings needed most in life, in order from the most important to the least. Obviously, the most important needs are the ones people have to have to survive, such as air, food, water, and shelter. Beyond that, however, was the need to belong and fit in with others. It is a powerful drive in humans and nowhere is that made clearer than in the typical high school, where differentness, as Midler calls it, is a curse.

I see "differentness" all the time in the school hallways and often, it carries a burden of unacceptance along with it. The kids that don't fit in because of their clothes, their background, or their behavior commonly struggle to mesh with the other students surrounding them. Others will go the opposite direction, fighting to be as unlike the average student as possible. Of course, when enough of them do that, they all find that suddenly, they belong to a group, albeit a group of "misfits."

When I first started high school, I was keenly aware of my own differentness and how it made it increasingly difficult to fit in with the groups that I wanted to be a part of. I was not beautiful enough to be a cheerleader, not smart enough to be an honors

student, not athletic enough to be a jock, and not wild enough to be a radical. It was a very lost and alone feeling and I felt almost a primitive level drive to change myself in some way so that I could merge with one of these groups. Instead, I found that there are a lot of us not that beautiful/smart/athletic/wild kids in school. These people are now my best friends. My differentness is not even apparent when I am with them because we all share that trait in one aspect or another. It has taught me that differentness is not right or wrong; it just is! Now I just hope that one day, like Midler, we will look back on our high school days and see just how our differentness made us the unique, special, and wonderful adults we are becoming.

Scoring evaluation: The student has a strong opinion on this issue and makes his or her points quite clear in an introduction, body, and conclusion format. Vocabulary use is very strong, and the use of the Maslow example ties in powerfully with the message in the essay. His or her personal examples also make each point stronger, and spelling and grammar are all error-free.

Score 5 Essay

I firmly believe that it is our "differentness" that makes us special. Even though being different is frowned upon in high school, I think that if we can hang on to our unique traits now, we will find, as Midler says, that later in life it is those very traits that will serve us best.

There is a strong push in our society, especially evident in high schools, toward conformity. If someone wears something outrageous to school, it is all everyone talks about. The student who doesn't like the same music as everyone else listens to, who eats weird things in the cafeteria, or who doesn't appear to have any interest in dating anyone on the football team/cheerleaders, is automatically suspect.

I am one of those nonconformists, I believe. Although I do not take it to the extreme like those students with dyed hair, multiple piercings, and nothing but black in their closets, I still am aware that I don't fit in with most of the people in my class. I would rather stay home with my family and go to one of the local museums than hang out at the mall. I am taller than most girls, but I am remotely athletic-minded. If I get some spare time between school and homework, I will usually pick up a sketchbook rather than a fashion magazine. My weekends are spent volunteering at the animal shelter and my favorite place to go is the arboretum just after they change the displays. Right now, this behavior labels me "weird" but I think that perhaps one day that will change and the label will read "fascinating."

Scoring evaluation: Although this is slightly shorter than the first essay, it is still quite strong. The examples are all good and relate directly to the test question. Vocabulary is good, and there are no spelling or grammar errors.

Score 4 Essay

Everybody is different in one way or another and that is the way it should be. A few months ago, I saw an old "Twilight Zone" episode that was supposed to take place in the future. In it, everyone looked the same. If you happened to look different, you were forced to have surgery. It made you look like the others. That was their definition of beauty. It was really interesting. I do not think that it was too impossible either. It's not a far-fetched idea for our culture at all.

Being different is natural but it is rarely easy. I find that I tend to hide my differentness from most people. I only feel like I can be myself when I am at home or with my two best friends. The other time, I try really hard just to be like everyone else. If you don't do this, people talk about you and I don't want that to happen to me.

Bette Midler says that it was her differentness that helped her become the famous person she is today. I have seen her on television and I bet she is right. Her looks are not typical and I bet her behavior wasn't either. Yet, today, those traits help to succeed. Perhaps that will happen to me too and the differentness that I have today will make me a more successful adult. I sure do like the idea.

Scoring evaluation: There is not a huge amount of development here, but the examples given are relevant. The sentence variety is limited with a lot of choppy sentences that could be improved. However, the student did a decent job of answering the question, providing some personal experiences for support and then bringing it to a conclusion by referring back to the original quote.

Score 3 Essay

Being different is just weird, I think. I mean, I see all these kids in school who are always trying to look different and they just come off looking stupid. What is the big deal about what you put on your body? Why does it have to carry some stupid brand name on it? I don't even pay attention to that stuff. Never have. I just get up and get dressed in whatever is clean.

Fitting in in high school is not easy, no matter what you do or wear, in my opinion. If you work hard to be different, it is even worse, in my opinion. I just try to keep my mouth shut, do my homework and get thru the day. I don't want to rock the boat and have people pay extra attention to me for anything. Being different gets attention. Don't want that. I will just stay quiet and wait until graduation. That's my opinion on it.

Scoring evaluation: There is a sincere attempt to answer the question here, but it gets lost somewhere along the way (perhaps in between all of those "my opinion" remarks). There is very little support for any points the student tries to make, and there are a number of fragments and usage errors.

Score 2 Essay

Everybody is different in some way or another. It is just part of life. Like snowflakes, you know? They are all different. That is what makes them pretty. At least, in my opinion. If we all looked and acted and talked and dressed and did the same things it would be boring, don't you think? So yes, different is good like in that old Burger King commershul. Remember that one?

Scoring evaluation: There are some things that could be used as a theme here, but the student drops them without any development. An opinion is listed but not supported, and then the student veered off topic completely.

Score 1 Essay

Feeling different. Not so bad. I feel it sumtimes. Don't care if I do. It's ok. They're are diffrent peopel everywhere. So what? Not right or wrong, just is.

Scoring evaluation: There is virtually nothing to redeem this essay other than the student did answer the test question. There are multiple errors that make it very hard to understand.

7. *"You can make more friends in two months by becoming interested in other people than you can in two years by trying to get other people interested in you."* —Dale Carnegie

   Assignment: Is Carnegie's idea the best way to make friends? Plan your response and support your position with specific points and examples from your observations, studies, reading, or personal experiences.

Score 6 Essay

Although I have never read this quote by Mr. Carnegie before, I have to say that I agree with it 100%. A year ago I might not have felt this way, but a recent event changed that.

For the last five years I have gone to a variety of camps. Some of them were church sponsored, while others had to do with Girl Scouts, 4-H, and Camp Fire Girls. Each time I would go hoping to make many new friends and each year, I came home disappointed. I had met some interesting people but no one that I truly connected with on a deep level. This past summer, that changed and it was all because of something my Grandma asked me. She drove me to camp and on the way asked me if I had any friends who also were attending. I explained my past failures at making those friends and she turned to me and asked a simple question: "When you meet someone new, what do you say to them?" I stumbled around and finally said that I told them about what movies and music I liked, what my school was like, and other details about me. Grandma chuckled and said, "That's no way to make friends. Why don't you ask them what movies and music they like?" I didn't know what to say. I had never even considered asking them questions before I introduced myself, but the idea had possibilities so I thought I'd try it.

What a difference it made! By approaching other girls at the camp and asking them simple questions (anything from where did you get that cute t-shirt to why don't you like mustard), they wanted to talk to me. It wasn't long before we were immersed in a conversation about each other and Mr. Carnegie's quote came true. If only we take the time to show interest in others, friendship cannot be far behind.

Scoring evaluation: This is a simple, but well-done essay. Although there are no profound vocabulary words and the sentence structure is fairly typical, the student does a great job of linking her personal experience with answering the question. The support is clear and understandable, and the format of introduction, body, and conclusion is very strong.

Score 5 Essay

I agree with Mr. Carnegie's statement but I think that it goes further than that. I believe that making friends is an important part of life that takes skill and dedication to maintain.

When I was in junior high, I was best friends with a girl named Molly. We did everything together, from sleepovers every weekend to signing up for the same summer art classes. We were inseparable and I thought we would stay that way for the rest of our lives. Unfortunately, high school disrupted those plans. During our first year, Molly joined the track team and suddenly, my closest friend was a complete stranger. She changed the way she talked, dressed, ate and acted so that she was just like the other girls on the team. We no longer appeared to have anything in common. I knew that she was doing these things in order to fit in with the other girls and be accepted by them and while I could understand her motives, I did not share them. Our friendship faded away quickly and today, Molly doesn't even acknowledge me when she sees me at school.

Although Molly is far more popular than I am in school now, I don't mind. I have spent my time cultivating two girls who are truly my best friends. We do everything together and throughout all of it, we are ourselves. We take a sincere interest in each other's interests while we maintain our individual uniqueness. To me, that is the key to real friendship.

Scoring evaluation: This is another strong essay, although it tends to ramble a little bit more than it should. The grammar and spelling are excellent, and the personal illustration supports the original test question. The three parts (introduction, body, and conclusion) are easy to see, and the sentence structure has good variety.

Score 4 Essay

In my personal opinion, I think that Mr. Dale Carnegie is exactly right about friendship. If you want to make friends, the key is to be interested in them and not the other way around. It makes sense. It probably works. I think I will try it sometime myself.

I recently went to a meeting with my mom and she put this suggestion into action right in front of me. She had been put in charge of the committee to raise money for repairing part of the library. She did not know anyone else on the committee. She was really nervous too. She was not sure what to say to them. She started by just reading the mission statement and other boring stuff. Then, she did something amazing. She stopped and asked each person to introduce him or herself to the rest of the group. With each person, she asked questions. They all lit up when she did that. She asked about their hobbies and jobs and other stuff. By the time everyone had done it, everyone was smiling and chatting. I told her she did a great job later.

I think what my mom did was exactly what Mr. Carnegie was recommending. It sure worked for her. In conclusion, I think that Mr. Carnegie was right and my mom was brilliant.

Scoring evaluation: This essay has some really good points. The example used to support the student's opinion is vivid and relevant. There is a definite introduction, body, and conclusion to the essay. The biggest flaws are lack of sentence variety and too much repetition.

Score 3 Essay

I can appreciate Mr. Carneig's advice but I don't know that I agree with it. If you are too interested in another person and ask them a lot of questions and stuff, you might have the cops called on you for harassing them. Maybe they will think you are a stalker or something. Scary stuff for sure.

Making friends, in my opinion, is all about finding out what you has in common. I like to play baseball and so does most of my friends, for example. I also like to fiddle around with ham radios and I've met some great guys in the local ham radio club. I met my best friend while we were both looking at graphic novels down at my favorite store. We like the same series which is *The Sandman* by Neil Gaiman. It has amazing stories of demons and wizards and other stuff in it.

Maybe I should learn to ask others about themselves more but then, I don't want the police after me, so maybe not. I think I will stick to the friends I already have. Other people can give Carngie's idea a try.

Scoring evaluation: This student answers the question and provides a personal experience example for support. A portion of the example is completely off topic, which hurts the essay as a whole. He also has verb tense and agreement errors, as well as spelling issues.

Score 2 Essay

I don't have a lot of friends. Wish I did though. Maybe I should stop talking about me and ask about them like that man Carnegie said in the quote on this test question. When me and my frinds get together though, we just don't do that much talking. We play some Playstation games and sometimes we go out and shoot some hoops. Talking is pretty rare. Is that wrong? I don't know. Maybe I could try it.

So, in conclusion and to summarize, I think that Carnegie was on the right track on the frend thing. I will keep it in mind.

Scoring evaluation: The student does answer the question in a way, and yet, it is lost amid the errors and the rambling about other things that do not tie to the main question. Although an introduction and body are primarily missing, he or she does try to put in a conclusion, although in a wordy and unnecessary way.

Score 1 Essay

Freinds are important. I have two good ones. Really good. Talk about stuff. Rode bikes and stuff. Gotta care bout the other one or it just don't work.

Carnegie got it good, I think. Agree with him. Freinds is just sumthin you got to have to make life more fun, ya know?

Scoring evaluation: As with most low scoring essays, this one is so riddled with errors that it is difficult to read. There are incomplete sentences, spelling errors, verb tense errors, and slang. There is no sense of organization and no examples to support an opinion.

9. *"How far you go in life depends on your being tender with the young, compassionate with the aged, sympathetic with the striving, and tolerant of the weak and the strong. Because someday in life you will have been all of these."*
—George Washington Carver

Assignment: How can relating to someone cause you to go far in life? Plan your response and support your position with specific points and examples from your observations, studies, reading, or personal experiences.

Score 6 Essay

There is an old saying that you should not begin to judge a person until you have walked in their shoes. In many ways, I think that this is what George Washington Carver was trying to say as well. It is important for all of us, as human beings, to be kind to others in other circumstances, because eventually we may find ourselves in this very same situation at some time in our life.

Carver reminds us that it is essential that not only are we gentle and compassionate to people who are younger, older, or struggling, but that doing so will influence what we achieve in the rest of our lives. This certainly reminds me of the familiar karmic saying of "what goes around, comes around." In other words, whatever you personally project out into the world is what you will eventually get in return. If we are empathetic to others, then when we are in need of kindness ourselves, it will be there one way or another.

Some who read Carver's quote may think that the phrase "how far you go in life" may refer to financial and/or professional success, but that is not how I perceived it at all. Instead, I feel as if Carver was trying to impart a more profound message: that our behavior toward other people from all walks of life is what will determine our own personal happiness. If this is indeed true, then it will change how I look at the entire world and perhaps that, after all, was what Carver was trying to convey.

Scoring evaluation: This is a great example of a student who is truly examining what a quote means. There is a lot of thought put into what he or she writes, along with great sentence variety; powerful supporting examples; excellent grammar and vocabulary; and a clear introduction, body, and conclusion.

Score 5 Essay

George Washington Carver's quote is an amazing philosophy to live by. I think that for anyone who lives in a very large city like I do, it has special meaning. Every single day I see homeless people standing on the corners downtown. They come in all shapes, sizes, and ages. They always look so sad and desolate that I look away because I don't know what else to do. Homelessness is such a huge issue in our city and it seems like no one has the right solution.

If I followed Carver's advice, however, perhaps looking away would be the worst thing I could do. Maybe, instead, I should take a moment to think about what it must be like to be in a situation like that and then respond with some kind of personal action. I have read that the best thing to do is donate some time to a homeless shelter or take in some of the items they need most like blankets, hats and gloves, and canned food. That would not be

too difficult to do and it could help a lot of people who need it.

By taking the time to help those who are in need, I might be able to help make the world a better place. If Carver is correct, it just might make me a better human being with a brighter future as well.

Scoring evaluation: Although this is a shorter essay, it is still very strong. The conclusion makes an obvious connection back to the introduction and the quote. The grammar, sentence structure, and vocabulary are all strong.

Score 4 Essay

I think that Carver is telling us we need to be nice to all kinds of people, the old, young, hurt, or weak. If we do that, you can go further in life and do better. I am not sure that is true, but it makes sense to me. I try to be nice to people that I meet.

I take care of my younger siblings a lot. That means I am nice to the younger. And to the weaker. I visit my grandparents a couple of times a month. I am always nice to them. I realize that I was once young and one day, I will be old too and I try to keep that in mind. Whether or not that will actually take me further in life, I don't know but it helps me to know that if I am nice to people now, then, hopefully, people will treat me nicely in the future.

Scoring evaluation: This student is trying to answer the question and does provide some supporting examples from his or her perspective. There is not much sentence variety and no outstanding vocabulary, but there is a semblance of an introduction, body, and conclusion.

Score 3 Essay

I disagree with Carver. That has nothing to do with how well you do in life. It may have to do with how much people like you. But it don't matter otherwise. How far you go in life is about work. Hard work. That is what my parents always tell me. So I work hard. I go to school. I have a part-time job after school.

Being nice to old people and young people is okay. I would not be mean. But I don't get what it has to do with success in life. You can't put it on a resume. Sure, some day you will be all those things. So what? It all goes back to working hard. I will have the money I need to take care of myself if I work hard enough. Carver was probly a nice person but he was all wrong about this one.

Scoring evaluation: This student definitely has an opinion on the matter and does use a little personal experience to support it; however, that is about the only thing done correctly. There are incomplete sentences; misspellings; and no sense of introduction, body, or conclusion.

Score 2 Essay

Carver is telling people to be nice to each other. Which is a great idea, by the way. I definitely agree with him. Everyone should agree with an idea like this one. He says be extra nice to old people and stuff like that. I am alwys extra nice to my grandma. She makes really good cookies too.

I guess he also says to be nice to little people plus really weak people. Like babies, maybe. Everyone knows that. Who would be mean to a baby? If you are, you should be locked up forever. See, Carver said so.

Scoring evaluation: There is an attempt to answer the question here, but there is little else that is good to say about it. The student fills up space by repeating unnecessary information. There is virtually nothing to support his or her opinion and no sense of introduction, body, or paragraph.

Score 1 Essay

I think hes tryin to say you better be nice. To everyone, yung, old, so on. If you don't, you will be really, really sorry. Bad things'll happen maybe. Carver was a smart guy. He new his stuff. Who is he anyway? Maybe I shud read something he wrote.

Scoring evaluation: The student actually did partially answer the question, but goes off topic, has no support or examples, and has no organization whatsoever.

14. *Aerodynamically, the bumble bee shouldn't be able to fly, but the bumble bee doesn't know it so it goes on flying anyway.* —Mary Kay Ash

> **Assignment:** What does this imply about the bee? How does this information then apply to people in general? Plan your response and support your position with specific points and examples from your observations, studies, reading, or personal experiences.

Score 6 Essay

I believe that this illustration of the bee is a reminder to each and every one of us that we truly can accomplish anything we want to in life as long as we believe that we can. The bee flies, not because nature designed it that way, but because it doesn't know that it can't. In the same vein, I believe that people can achieve miraculous things, not because of their genetics, but because they have the self-confidence and inner drive to reach their goals.

Examples of this philosophy can be found everywhere we look. People are determined to lose weight, quit smoking, run a marathon, or go back to school or any of hundreds of personal ambitions. They do this because they firmly believe they can. A philosophy like this can literally transform your life. It opens the doors to endless possibilities and virtually eliminates the concept of "I can't." What a wonderful way to approach life!

One of my favorite songs has a line in it which states, "Imagine what you would do if you knew you could not fail." That always makes me stop and think because so many times, I believe we are held back by nothing other than fear of failure. Why bother joining the debate team? We will never be able to hold our own in an argument. Why take the time to exercise? We will just gain the weight back. Why study? We will just screw up the test. This line of thinking is dangerous; it can lead to a descending spiral of such negative thinking that soon we cannot get out of our beds in the morning. I have seen this happen to someone close to me and it was a wake-up call for me and how I looked at my own future. It taught me a vital lesson about what I can expect. Now, I hope to approach life with the same attitude as that bumble bee. Of course I can fly! As long as I believe I can and no one tries to tell me otherwise, I plan to soar!

Scoring evaluation: This essay perfectly shows how a student can answer a question using a clear introduction, body, and conclusion, with relevant examples and personal experiences. Grammar, spelling, and vocabulary are excellent with strong sentence variety. Note how well the student maintained the right pronouns (*we/us*) throughout the essay.

Score 5 Essay

The bumble bee flies because it has never been told that it cannot do so. I think this is a great idea for everyone to adopt in their own lives. Just imagine what humans could do if they had never been told it was impossible!

History is full of examples of people who have done what others told them was simply impossible. Susan B. Anthony campaigned for voting rights for women when her culture told her she was crazy. The Wright Brothers pursued human flight when others thought it would never happen. Helen Keller went after a full education and career even though she was deaf, mute, and blind. I am sure many told her that it was impossible.

Even I have come up against times where people have told me something was impossible but I didn't listen. When I decided to try out for the track team, my brothers laughed at me. They said I would never make it because I was too klutzy. Were they ever surprised when I set a new record in sprints last

spring! I sure am glad that I ignored them and concentrated on just doing my best instead.

What makes something possible in life is the sheer determination to make it happen. That is what spurred on people like Anthony, the Wrights, and Keller—and me. All of us were completely dedicated to accomplishing something and we did it. The same is true for all of us. All we have to do is decide that we want to achieve something and who knows how far it may take us? Perhaps we won't achieve exactly what we had set out to, but as the old saying goes, "Shoot for the moon. Even if you miss, you'll land among the stars." And the stars would not be too bad a place to be, right? Maybe we will spot a bumble bee flying past!

Scoring evaluation: This is another strong essay with a great tie in between the introduction and conclusion. It has relevant examples from history, as well as from personal experience. This essay uses a little more repetition than it should and sentence variety could be improved a little, but otherwise an excellent example of how to write an essay.

Score 4 Essay

While I think this is a wonderful thing for bumble bees, I don't see how it applies to human beings at all. Animals often can do things that scientists do not understand but it is not because they are determined or anything like that. As animals, they are not capable of higher thinking like that. Only humans have that ability.

We stop ourselves from doing things that seem impossible because we are able to reason things out, rather than just be guided by genetics and instinct. Right? That makes sense. So, while bees may be able to fly even though science says they cannot, we are different. We listen to what the scientists tell us about what is possible. And what is not. That is for our own safety. If we thought we could fly, a lot of us would be jumping off cliffs and skyscrapers and finding out the hard way that it really was impossible after all. What lesson would you learn then?

Let those bees keep flying. Ignorant of the fact that they can't. In the meantime, I will keep my feet on the ground and if someone told me something is not possible, I will listen carefully. Who knows? They may be wrong but I won't risk hurting or even killing myself to find out, you know?

Scoring evaluation: This student has a very valid point. He or she disagrees that the quote applies to humans (remember that you are NOT scored on if you agree or disagree) and has some relevant support in the examples used. There are some spelling and grammatical errors and a lot of repetition/wordiness. There are some problems with pronoun shifting and verb tense issues as well.

Score 3 Essay

Bumble bees are pretty neat insects. I am not surprised to find out that they are not supposed to be able to fly, but they still do. They seem like determened creatures to me. I think that the quote is basically saying that you can do anything you want if I want to enough. That is a nice idea and I hope that it is true.

Of course, there are limits. I mean, people may want to be able to fly, but they can't, right? I would like to live on the other side of the country, but I don't see that happening anytime soon either. So, while the bee idea is a nice one, I think it has to have alot of limits on it.

I guess the answer is to just keep trying. Don't give up. That is what my parents are always telling me at least. They keep telling me to just hang in there and not give up when I am struggling with my homework or practecing my piano. Think I must be as determened as a bee, I guess.

Scoring evaluation: Although there is an attempt to answer the question here, it rambles quite a bit and has a number of errors in it. There is no real insight into the question and too much slang or informal language. The organization is very loose, and there is a lot of repetition.

Score 2 Essay

Bees fly like people walk. It is what they do. I don't know if they have to know how it works to be able to do it. I don't know how I walk. It just happens. I imagine that it how it is with bees too.

Science is strange. I don't always understand it. Not my favorite class at all. I can ask my teacher. Explain it to me so that I understand why bees can really fly.

Scoring evaluation: The student is responding to the question without any clear opinion, supporting examples, or a sense of organization. He or she misses the objective of answering the essay prompt with his or her own opinion, which is evident in the "don't know" and "don't understand" statements. In the second paragraph, the student veers off topic completely.

Score 1 Essay

This is dumb. Bees wouldn't understand it anyway. Bees fly. They want to. Why not? What else would they do. I don't get it. Who said this? Probly scientist.

Applies to people. No clue. Just bees, right? Keep flying is all they can do.

Scoring evaluation: The student clearly does not get the point of the quote and is unable to write anything in the essay. There are too many mistakes to be able to read it, no examples, and no organization.

17. *"Are you bored with life? Then throw yourself into some work you believe in with all your heart, live for it, die for it, and you will find happiness that you had thought could never be yours."* —Dale Carnegie

> **Assignment:** Do you agree or disagree that this is the best solution to boredom? Plan your response and support your position with specific points and examples from your observations, studies, reading, or personal experiences.

Score 6 Essay

The concept of finding happiness through work is not one that you hear promoted very often in today's culture. Instead, jobs are something that we tolerate, a necessary evil in life. What a breath of fresh air to learn Mr. Carnegie's opinion instead. I have every intention of spending my life immersed in a type of work that brings me fulfillment, happiness and yes, an end to boredom.

Boredom is a natural part of life and can often be the springboard that you need to discover something new and exciting. My mother always told me the same thing whenever I told her that I was bored. She would respond with, "How wonderful for you! What amazing things might you find out today?" She frequently reminded me that boredom is a gift; people who are struggling to survive rarely have the time or luxury to be bored. I did not appreciate her input as much as I should have then; I do now.

I believe the key to spending too much of your time mired in boredom is simply finding something that fascinates you and pursue it. Who knows how far it may take you? You never know what direction it may lead. For example, when I was younger, I commonly complained of being bored during the summer. One night (probably to just shut me up!), my mom took me to the local community theater to see a play. I was enthralled by live theater. Watching live performances only a few rows away was absolutely thrilling for me and became a personal obsession. To help support my love of theater, my parents had me volunteer at the community theater as an usher. I ushered for three years and although you would think I was primarily interested in becoming an actor, my biggest passion was in watching the theater's choreographer teaching dance steps. One day, he noticed my interest and before long, he was telling me how he became a choreographer. Two years later, I am taking three dance classes and am looking seriously at a career teaching other dancers.

Hidden in between each step I take is that sparkle of boredom that fueled the discovery. I found it and know that, without a doubt, it led to my happiness.

Scoring evaluation: This student clearly responds to the test question and does it in a clear, organized fashion. Sentence variety is excellent as is use of vocabulary. His or her personal experiences relate directly to the topic and are given with strong supporting details. He or she definitely provided personal insight into the issue in a very strong essay.

Score 5 Essay

Being bored with life is a ridiculous notion to me. With all there is to discover, how can anyone have the chance to be bored? I think boredom is usually either a sign of laziness or ignorance.

I have seen many kids my age bored. They are bored all summer when school is out. They are bored sitting in the classroom. They are bored hanging out at the mall. They are bored while talking to each other on the phone. I have to wonder why it is so different for me. Why am I not bored like them? I think the answer lies in the fact that I have a lot of hobbies. Some kids tease me about it, but those hobbies keep my mind active and boredom is just never an issue.

The free time I have after school and on weekends is usually spent on one of these hobbies. For example, I do a lot of drawing. I spend a great deal of time outside with my sketch pad, drawing whatever comes to mind. I keep a journal, so sometimes, when I am done sketching, I will write in it. Another hobby is that my volunteer job at the local retirement center. I spend about 15 hours a month there reading out loud to some of the residents. They seem to like it and I've made some really great friends there.

I truly believe that boredom comes from a lack of thinking of other things to do. If other kids would just think about hobbies to start, places to volunteer, and interesting things to learn how to do, boredom would disappear and happiness would be guaranteed!

Scoring evaluation: This student takes a completely different perspective on the question but responds very well with relevant personal examples and good organization. There is some repetitive sentence structure and vocabulary, but for the most part, this is a strong and well-done essay.

Score 4 Essay

Being bored is rarely fun. It can lead to some fun things though. For example, one time I was really bored while I was sitting in the car waiting for my mom to come back out of the grocery store. While I was there, I was watching this man plant flowers in the store's side lot. He was right next to our car. I didn't have anything to do, so I started chatting with him through the window. He was nice. He worked for a landscaping company. They plants flowers, plants and trees for businesses and home owners. He had been doing it for more than 20 years. After I had asked a lot of questions, he wanted to know why I was so interested. I told him I liked doing outdoor work. By the time my mom came back from the store, we were already talking about my working as a volunteer at his landscaping company. Mom liked

the idea. She thought it sounded like a good thing to do. So now, two months later. I'm still helping out. In the summer, they are going to start paying me. Being bored led me to a really fun job. Who would have ever thought that?

Scoring evaluation: Along with being too short, this essay makes the mistake of running everything together. While there may be a sense of organization, it is lost in this formatting. Sentence variety is quite limited, and there is a great deal of repetition. The student did answer the question and use a personal experience as support for his or her opinion.

Score 3 Essay

Mr. Dale Carnegie said that if you are bored with life, you should find some kind of work that you like and pour yourself into it. He said to pick something you would put your heart into. He said that you would be happy then.

I guess he is right. I guess that if you found something like that, you could be happy. I think it would be hard to find though. I think many people search of it all of there lives really. I know my parents talk about getting jobs he would like better but not sure what.

Mr. Dale Carnegie was a smart man, I bet. Advice sounds good. I will tell my parents what he said. Could help, maybe. Wouldn't that be nice?

So, in my opinion, Mr. Dale Carnegie is right about what he said about boredom. That is the conclusion I came to after reading his quote.

Scoring evaluation: This student is using a common technique to make the essay longer. The first paragraph is nothing but a repeat of the test question (only without sentence variety). There is a great deal of repetition in the second paragraph, although it is an attempt to provide a personal experience example for support. The ending is another example of trying to make the essay longer without actually saying a word.

Score 2 Essay

Boredom is aweful. It happens to me almost every single day. I think it's pretty normal, right? I suppose finding something inneresting would be a good thing to do but I can never come up with nothing. My sister always picks up a book. But that is too much like homework for me. My parents are giving me chore's. I don't like that too.

The man says to throw yourself into sumthin. Like what? I need ideas. Hate being bored. I sick of it really. Guess I could go outside. Rains a lot. No, I think, in my opinion, in conclusion, that boredom is turrible but a part of life. We all deal with.

Scoring evaluation: The student is responding to the question, but without any clear sense of an opinion and so full of errors, it is hard to figure out what is being said. In the end, he or she tries to make the essay longer by throwing in "I think, in my opinion, in conclusion," which is a sure sign to all scorers that this student has nothing to truly say.

Score 1 Essay

Well, who is'nt bored now and then? Part of life. Work sure aren't the anser either. If I am bored I just go to sleep. Or call my frends. I can talk for hours. Maybe I just don't get it. Why is this Carngie guy saying you should work if your bored? No sense in that. So, in conclusion, I guess I think he's wrong. Is that ok?

Scoring evaluation: The student has pretty much missed the whole point of this quote. His or her response is so hard to read because of the errors that the essay could not possibly get more than a 1. There are spelling errors, grammar errors, off-topic responses, and absolutely no sense of organization or supporting examples.

Responding to Idea Prompts

Read through and answer the following practice writing prompts, giving yourself about 25 minutes for each essay. Remember, there is no right or wrong argument, but make sure you stay on topic.

1. Many people believe that television is extremely educational and a vital part of keeping up with today's world. Others feel that it is a negative influence, especially on youth. They think it can lead to violence, apathy, and stunted brain growth.

   Assignment: Do you think television has helped or hurt our culture? Plan your response and support your position with specific points and examples from your observations, studies, reading, or personal experiences.

2. As automobile manufacturers struggle to make their products more fuel efficient and environmentally safe, a growing number of people are advocating giving up cars altogether in favor of bicycles. They believe that they are the better mode of transportation, saving gas, avoiding pollution, and providing exercise all at the same time.

   Assignment: Would the world improve if more people used bicycles instead of cars? Plan your response and support your position with specific points and examples from your observations, studies, reading, or personal experiences.

3. According to some people, elderly drivers should be required to reapply for their driving licenses because with age comes diminished vision, hearing, and reaction time. This, in turn, can mean bigger threats to the older drivers, as well as to the drivers around them. Many elderly drivers, however, require driving licenses for day-to-day activities, like grocery shopping or doctor appointments.

   Assignment: Do you think that elderly drivers should be tested more often the usual driver? What age do you think is best? What boundaries would you set for allowing them to get or not get their licenses renewed? Plan your response and support your position with specific points and examples from your observations, studies, reading, or personal experiences.

4. Many parents give children a weekly or monthly allowance regardless of their behavior because they believe an allowance teaches children to be financially responsible. Other parents only give children an allowance as a reward for completing chores or when they have behaved properly.

   Assignment: Which method do you think teaches children the best lesson? Plan your response and support your position with specific points and examples from your observations, studies, reading, or personal experiences.

5. It is becoming abundantly clear that males and females learn in different ways. In response to this, a few model schools are separating the sexes so that classes are all one gender. By doing this, the teacher can focus on teaching to that sex's primary learning styles.

   Assignment: Do you think separating boys and girls into different classrooms is the right way to go? Plan your response and support your position with specific points and examples from your observations, studies, reading, or personal experiences.

6. Many schools offer students who are native speakers of another language the opportunity to take classes in their native tongue so that they can more easily assimilate and better understand the material. Some educators believe that this is a disservice and that these students should be immersed in the English language.

> **Assignment:** Do you think immersion should be mandatory for students who are native speakers of another language? Plan your response and support your position with specific points and examples from your observations, studies, reading, or personal experiences.

7. Many people feel that the use of surveillance cameras in public places, such as parking lots, is a good idea that can help ensure our safety. Others worry that too many cameras violate our right to privacy and give law enforcement officials too much power.

> **Assignment:** Is installing more surveillance cameras in public places a matter of safety or privacy? Plan your response and support your position with specific points and examples from your observations, studies, reading, or personal experiences.

8. When people go shopping, some go to the larger department/chain stores. These stores often have the lowest prices and widest selection of products. On the other hand, some shoppers specifically try to shop at small, locally owned businesses instead. They may have to pay more, but feel they are supporting their community in the process.

> **Assignment:** Which shopper would you agree or disagree with? Plan your response and support your position with specific points and examples from your observations, studies, reading, or personal experiences.

9. Today's top professional athletes often have salaries and bonuses in the tens of millions of dollars. Golfer Tiger Woods makes more than $80 million per year and football pro Peyton Manning makes over $42 million.

> **Assignment:** Do you think these athletes deserve such high compensation? Plan your response and support your position with specific points and examples from your observations, studies, reading, or personal experiences.

10. Many people believe that competition is a natural part of life and belongs in the public school system. Students regularly compete in everything from the football team and the debate team to choir contests and even in grades. Others believe that competition is harmful and discouraging to students and should be de-emphasized, while lessons on teamwork and cooperation are encouraged instead.

> **Assignment:** Which opinion do you agree with the most? Plan your response and support your position with specific points and examples from your observations, studies, reading, or personal experiences.

11. According to the National Center for Statistics and Analysis of the National Highway Traffic Safety Administration, at any given moment during the day, 974,000 cars on the road are being driven by a person talking on a cell phone. Some states have made it illegal to do this. Other states are giving the idea some thought.

> **Assignment:** Should it be illegal for the driver of a vehicle to use a cell phone? Plan your response and support your position with specific points and examples from your observations, studies, reading, or personal experiences.

12. Many albums and CDs now contain stickers warning parents that the lyrics of some of the songs may not be suitable for children. Some people argue that simply putting a sticker on a label is not enough. Others think it is an infringement on the freedom of speech to put a label on a CD at all.

> **Assignment:** Are these inappropriate lyrics warnings necessary? Plan your response and support your position with specific points and examples from your observations, studies, reading, or personal experiences.

13. For decades, elementary school students across the country have been required to stand up and say the Pledge of Allegiance to the American flag. That practice has recently been called into question, and now, standing and reciting the pledge is optional.

> **Assignment:** Should students be required to say the pledge, should it remain optional, or should the practice be completely halted? Plan your response and support your position with specific points and examples from your observations, studies, reading, or personal experiences.

14. Many junior high and high schools around the country require their students to spend a certain number of hours doing volunteer work or community service. Some people believe that this is an excellent idea that promotes good citizenship and cultivates compassion. Others feel that forced volunteerism is not actually volunteerism at all.

> **Assignment:** Which opinion do you agree with in this issue? Plan your response and support your position with specific points and examples from your observations, studies, reading, or personal experiences.

15. Today, more and more colleges and universities are offering not only individual courses but entire degree programs online. Some educators worry that online programs do not provide the same quality as an on-campus education and that in an online program, students can get others to do their work. Others believe online courses offer convenience and flexibility, which enables students, who might otherwise not be able, to earn a degree and complete their educations.

> **Assignment:** Should colleges and universities offer degrees entirely online? Plan your response and support your position with specific points and examples from your observations, studies, reading, or personal experiences.

16. Personal computers are a part of most schools and homes today. Students spend hours every day at the keyboard doing homework, talking to friends, downloading music, printing papers, and more. Some experts worry that young people are spending too much time on the computer and advise parents to limit the time to no more than three hours a day.

> **Assignment:** Do you believe that computer time should be restricted? Plan your response and support your position with specific points and examples from your observations, studies, reading, or personal experiences.

17. Many schools employ security guards and have installed security equipment such as video cameras and metal detectors in the building. Police have brought in dogs to sniff out drugs, and lockers are sometimes searched randomly. The schools believe that these steps are necessary in order to maintain safety, but some students feel like they are attending a prison instead of a school.

> **Assignment:** Are security measures in schools necessary? Plan your response and support your position with specific points and examples from your observations, studies, reading, or personal experiences.

18. One of the biggest educational trends in recent years is homeschooling. It is growing each year by approximately 15%. More than one million children of all ages are currently being educated at home.

> **Assignment:** Do you think that homeschooling is a valuable educational method? Plan your response and support your position with specific points and examples from your observations, studies, reading, or personal experiences.

19. Many cities suffer from serious air and noise pollution—as well as endless traffic jams—because of too many cars. Some people feel that cities with extensive public transportation systems should ban passenger cars and force people to walk, bike, or use public transportation.

> **Assignment:** Should the number of passenger cars be limited by law? Plan your response and support your position with specific points and examples from your observations, studies, reading, or personal experiences.

20. According to some health organizations, many foods on the grocery store shelves are made with generically modified ingredients. This process helps reduce susceptibility to disease, improve flavor, and reduce overall costs. Most of these foods, however, do not have a genetically modified organism (GMO) label.

> **Assignment:** Should laws require manufacturers to label foods containing GMOs? Plan your response and support your position with specific points and examples from your observations, studies, reading, or personal experiences.

► Scoring Guide and Sample Essays

These types of writing essays are graded in the same way as the quotation-based essays. Refer to Chapter 5 for detailed scoring guidelines.

Sample Essays

4. Many parents give children a weekly or monthly allowance regardless of their behavior because they believe an allowance teaches children to be financially responsible. Other parents only give children an allowance as a reward for completing chores or when they have behaved properly.

> **Assignment:** Which method do you think teaches children the best lesson? Plan your response and support your position with specific points and examples from your observations, studies, reading, or personal experiences.

Score 6 Essay

Starting when I was about eight years old, my parents gave me a list of chores that had to be completed each week. If I did my chores, I got an allowance, a bit of change that I could use as I pleased. If I didn't do my chores, I didn't get my allowance. There was no other punishment, but no other punishment was necessary. That dollar or two a week was all the incentive I needed to help out around the house. Whether it was the latest Barbie or a six-pack of Hubba Bubba chewing gum, there was always something I wanted to buy. My parents could always count on me doing my chores.

I think that giving children an allowance for doing chores is a smart parenting move, for it accomplishes four important goals: It helps ensure that important work gets done around the house; it teaches children that they need to do their part

to make things run smoothly for the whole family; it rewards children in a realistic, practical way for good behavior; and it helps teach children how to handle money.

I know that some people consider money for chores a form of bribery, and others feel that children should just do their chores anyway, without the incentive of an allowance. They argue that giving kids money for doing chores undermines the lesson that they need to help the family and do their part. I can understand that point of view, and when parents give their children too much money, it does undermine those lessons. But when the allowance is small, it is simply a modern version of the age-old practice of rewarding good behavior. Once children reach a certain age, money is an appropriate and effective reward that helps them learn how to be responsible and how to manage money. They get a sense of what things are worth and how much they have to save and spend to get what they want. And learning to save in order to purchase a desired item teaches them patience and helps children better understand the value of hard work.

Giving children money for doing chores is also a good introduction to the reality of the workplace. If they do the work, they get paid; if they don't do the work, they don't. Extra work can be rewarded with bonuses and extra praise; poor work may result in a pay cut or demotion.

It's important for parents to find the right amount to give. Too much money may make a child feel like hired help and will undermine the goal of teaching children to help simply because they are part of a family that must work together. On the other hand, too little money may make a child feel resentful, as if his or her work isn't worth anything to the household. What's an appropriate amount? It depends upon the amount of chores the child is expected to do and the child's age. If your nine-year-old is only expected to clean his or her room, a dollar a week is probably plenty. If your 14-year-old is expected to keep his room clean, take out the trash, water the plants, and vacuum the house, then ten dollars a week is more appropriate.

Being paid for my chores helped me have a good attitude about housework, taught me how to save money and spend it wisely, and enabled me to appreciate the hard work my parents did around the house. I'm really grateful that this was the way my parents chose to handle chores in our household.

Scoring evaluation: This essay receives the maximum score for apparent reasons. It takes a stance (giving kids allowances for chores done) and then supports it with clear and relevant examples from the student's personal life. Each point is strongly presented with logical and clear points; the grammar and vocabulary are error-free; the length is longer than some but would fit depending on the handwriting style. There is a clear introduction, body, and conclusion to the essay, and it stays on topic from beginning to end.

Score 5 Essay

I think that giving children an allowance based solely on their behavior is a huge mistake. The lesson the kids will take away from this is not the one most that parents truly want to impart.

When I was younger, I was jealous of my cousins because they received a regular allowance. In my household, this was not the case. We were expected to do certain chores, of course, but there was no compensation for it other than appreciation. If we needed money for something, we had to tell our parents what it was and why we felt it was important for us to purchase it. It was amazing how silly some of the items sounded when actually described in detail to a parent.

While I was over at my cousin's house one afternoon, I listened enviously as my cousins told me the different things they had bought with their allowance. They did not have to do any work around the house to earn it. They did not have to justify

their wants at all. They simply used the money as they wanted to. That sounded great to me. As I was writing my speech to convince my parents in my mind, my two younger cousins began to argue. Just then, my Aunt Nancy came in and said, "Do you two want an allowance this week or not?" Both of them smiled at each other and said, "Sorry!" The minute their mom was out of the room, however, they went right back to bickering. It was immediately clear to me that they only pretended to make up because their allowance depended on it, not because they truly felt remorseful. That seemed wrong to me.

I began thinking about it and I decided that paying children for good behavior is wrong. Good behavior is something that is its own reward and to put a price tag on it removes the essential lessons it should provide. If parents want to give their children an allowance, I believe it should be unrelated to their behavior and instead, just given as a gift for being part of the family. This is what I plan to do with my own children in the future.

Scoring evaluation: This is another excellent response to the writing prompt. It is somewhat shorter but still has a clear introduction, body, and conclusion. The student's point of view is clearly stated (allowances given for behavior is a mistake), and her personal anecdote supports her opinion. The vocabulary is not quite as strong as in a level 6 essay, but still good. The grammar is good, and the length is appropriate.

Score 4 Essay

Should parents pay children for doing chores is a good question. My parents paid me, and my brothers and sister. I never liked doing chores, but getting an allowance each week (if I did my chores) made it not so bad. In fact, sometimes I did extra (like reorganizing the pantry) to get some extra money for something I really wanted.

I think having my allowance depend on my doing chores made me understand what it's like to work.

In the "Real World," you don't get paid if you don't do your work. That's how it was in our house.

I also learned that it's hard work to keep a house going, I learned to appreciate all the hard work my mom and dad use to do. In addition, I learned how to save money. I would set aside my allowance to save up for something I wanted, like a new CD player or outfit.

In my opinion, parents should give an allowance for doing chores, but it shouldn't be too much. Children should know that they need to help no matter what. Too much money I think would make him or her feel like their hired help or something. Contrarily, too little money can make him or her feel like their help isn't worth anything to his or her parents. So finding the right amount is important.

In conclusion, giving children an allowance for doing household chores is a good idea. Children learn to work for their money and save what they earn.

Scoring evaluation: Although the student has a strong viewpoint and supports it with relevant examples, the vocabulary is weaker here, with a lot of repetition. Sentence variety is limited, and there are several grammar and usage errors. It is also on the short side, coming in at just about 250 words when the ideal is 350 to 450.

Score 3 Essay

I think allowances are a bad thing for kids. They do not learn responsibility like parents think they will. They just learn to spend money on stupid things.

In my family, allowances are not even up for discussion. My dad would just say forget it. No way. He thinks that we should just do things around the house because that is being part of a family. I guess that he is right in some ways accept I would really enjoy having my own cash now and then.

Children should behave well. They should do what they are told. They should listen to their parents. They should not except money for it either.

Perhaps the best answer is giving kids spending money occasionally so that they can purchase what they want. The mistake is in tying it to certain kinds of behavior. I think it is really wrong.

Scoring evaluation: This essay tends to use choppier sentences and overly informal, slang terms. It is far too short, and there are some basic errors like word choice (*accept/except* and *except/expect*). The vocabulary is limited, and there is little to no insight into the question that was asked.

Score 2 Essay

Allowances, they are cool. I always loved getting mine. I plan to give my kids their own allowances someday too. I think it gives them some freedom. And it teaches them about how to take care of money.

I usually got an allowance no matter what I did or did not do. That probly didn't teach me the best lessons, I usually spent it on stupid things that would either break or get lost in just a few days.

It must be tough for parents to make a decision like this. They have to weigh a lot of different factors. Of course, parenting is full of tough decisions. That is one reason I do not plan to have any kids for a very long time.

Allowances are a good idea. I would give one to my kids if they would take the trash out for me. That is the one chore I always hated the most.

Scoring evaluation: Although this student made an effort to fill up the lines, there are many errors in the essay, including spelling. There is no sentence variety, and most of the essay tends to stray off topic.

Score 1 Essay

Many children they do not behave in properly, they should be punish, no getting reward. They should no be allowance anything. Chores is hard, on the contrary, there to learn for helping that's important. For the family. All to do the parts.

For me, it was vacuuming and the dusting. Every week, for Saturday or else. Forgetting the allowance, there wasn't. Only to be punish for what not to do.

Children should listen, to their parents. Its very important.

Scoring evaluation: There is little right in this essay. Verb tenses, punctuation, and spelling are all incorrect. Because there are so many errors, it would be hard for a scorer to read and understand what is being said.

7. Many people feel that the use of surveillance cameras in public places, such as parking lots, is a good idea that can help ensure our safety. Others worry that too many cameras violate our right to privacy and give law enforcement officials too much power.

> **Assignment:** Is installing more surveillance cameras in public places a matter of safety or privacy? Plan your response and support your position with specific points and examples from your observations, studies, reading, or personal experiences.

Score 6 Essay

Not long ago, the nation was gripped by the horrifying news that a baby had been stolen from a car in a parking lot while her mother, who was returning a shopping cart, was just a few feet away. Thanks to the description of the kidnapper captured by surveillance cameras in the parking lot and broadcast over radios, television, and highway overpass signs, the kidnapper was quickly caught and the baby returned, unharmed, to her mother. Had it not been for those surveillance cameras, that mother would probably never have seen her baby girl again.

I can't think of a much better argument for the use of surveillance cameras in public places. That baby's life was saved by those parking lot cameras.

Many people worry about the use of surveillance cameras in public places such as parking lots, stores, parks, and roadways. They don't like the idea that they are being watched. They worry that the information captured on the surveillance tapes can somehow be used against them. But how? It seems to me that the only reason we should worry about being caught on surveillance cameras is if we are doing something wrong. If we are behaving lawfully in a public place, then why worry if it is captured on film?

Surveillance cameras can provide two immensely important services. One, they can help us find those who commit crimes, including thieves, kidnappers, vandals, and even murderers. Two, they can serve as a powerful deterrent to crime. A thief who plans to steal a car may think twice if he knows he will be caught on video. A woman who hopes to kidnap a child may abandon her plans if she knows she will be captured on film.

Surveillance cameras can also help us in less critical but nonetheless practical ways. In some towns in England, for example, radio deejays use information from surveillance cameras to announce the availability of parking spaces in crowded public parking lots. Problems of all shapes and sizes can also be noted and addressed through video surveillance. For example, imagine a video camera installed in a local town square. Reviewing the films, officials might realize that people who meet in the square move quickly into the shade of the one tree in the center of the square. This could move officials to plant more trees or provide tables with umbrellas so that people could meet and relax in the shade. Similarly, a video camera in a grocery store might reveal that Aisle 7 is always overcrowded, prompting the manager to re-arrange items to more evenly distribute shoppers.

Of course it's possible to have too much of a good thing, and if surveillance cameras cross the line and start being installed on private property—that is, in our offices and homes—then we will have the "Big Brother is watching" scenario opponents fear. If that were the case, I would be against surveillance cameras, too. But as long as surveillance cameras are limited to public places, they can help ensure our safety.

Scoring evaluation: This essay does it all: It has sentence variety; powerful and relevant examples; a clear (and grabbing!) introduction, body, and conclusion; and an excellent use of vocabulary. The student even looks briefly at the opposite side of the issue and shows why it is understandable, but not logical.

Score 5 Essay

While I do understand that surveillance cameras have many practical purposes in today's world, I still find the very notion of them disturbing and unnerving. It is too easy to slip over the line between necessary and invasive. That line is just too thin.

While I realize that many of the surveillance cameras are installed in buildings for sound reasons, the idea that I am being watched as I walk through a store, across a parking lot or into a city bus is unpleasant. I find myself feeling guilty and self-conscious when I have no logical reason for it. It is similar to the feeling I get when a police car is behind me during traffic. I almost adopt suspicious behavior—fidgeting with my hair, glancing repeatedly at the cameras and shifting from one position to another—and just because I know that perhaps somewhere someone is watching my every move.

Because surveillance equipment is so common, I also worry that it will be used improperly, either commercially or personally. I fear that these cameras will be put in places that are truly unnecessary, whether it be public restrooms, store dressing rooms or club locker rooms. While it sounds unlikely, I suspect that some people would find a way to explain the necessity of these particular cameras, one way or another.

While a minimal number of surveillance equipment truly is necessary in a violent and crime-filled world as ours, I think there should be a plethora of

requirements and red tape to fulfill before they can be utilized. If not, regular, law-abiding, honest citizens such as myself will continue to worry that they are being watched by "Big Brother" at all, and frequently inappropriate, times.

Scoring evaluation: This essay does a good job of taking a position and explaining it. There are not as many strong examples, but all of the requirements are here: sentence variety, strong vocabulary, good grammar and usage skills, and an ability to concisely express thoughts and feelings. The conclusion is solid and ties back to the opening paragraph.

Score 4 Essay

Many public places now have surveillance cameras, the main reason being to ensure safety. I think this is a good idea, and that more places should have them.

Surveillance cameras are a good thing because they help keep us safe. If people know they might be on video then, they probably won't do something bad or against the law, like stealing. This is a big protection for us. It makes me feel safer, especially like in a parking lot in the night time. The other good thing about surveillance cameras, is that they can help us catch someone who does do something bad. For example, stealing a car in a parking lot. The camera can get a good picture of the thief and the police will have a good description of the person who stole the car. That makes it a lot easier to catch the thief.

I think surveillance cameras can also be used for other good things, like helping fix traffic jams in grocery stores. I mean if you can see that people are always crowding in one isle, for example.

I know that some people are upset about this kind of thing (being on film) and think that it's like "Big Brother is watching," or something. Also, some people just don't like being on cameras. However, if you're not doing anything wrong, it shouldn't matter.

Their only for finding people who do things wrong. To me, I think that makes a lot of sense.

Scoring evaluation: This student gives it a good try, but falls short in several areas. There is a lot of repetition, and the examples cited do not sufficiently support his viewpoint. There are some grammar errors (fragments, etc.), and the essay shifts pronouns often, from *they* and *people* to *me* and *us*. It is also too short.

Score 3 Essay

Surveillance cameras are important. They are the key evidence in capturing crooks and other criminals. How many times have you turned on the television and seen endless replays of the latest tape catching someone in the act of committing a crime? Grainy black and white pictures leads to going to trial. Eventually, prison.

Of course these cameras invade privacy. That is not even up for debate. It is obvious. The thing people have to figure out is if some lost of privacy is worth more safety. I believe that the majority of people would say yes. It is definitely worth it.

Recently, I was grateful for surveillance cameras. When some illegal activity occurred in the school parking lot (I won't say what it was) my name was turned in for doing it. I made it very clear that I was not a part of it. But I was not let go until the surveillance tape was viewed several times. That tape made it clear. I was not a part of the deal. That was cool.

I do not like the idea of being watched all the time. No one does. It feels creepy. But it has its points. In conclusion, these cameras can be really important. I think we should have more of them.

Scoring evaluation: The student tried hard to fill out all of the lines, but in doing so, used choppy sentences and a great deal of repetition, plus the writer waffles on viewpoint (from negative to positive and vice versa). There is little vocabulary development and very little insight into the actual question.

Score 2 Essay

Should we install survellance cameras in more public places or not. That is an excellent question. It is a good think to think about. It is important.

These cameras watch people. I guess they watch me sometimes, I never noticed. I will keep an eye out for them more often now. I wonder if they are in alot of places. I bet they catch crimenals. They seem to pop up on tv all the time.

So I guess that more of these cameras would be ok. They just better not put them in places where people change close and stuff.

Scoring evaluation: This essay takes a lot of space to say virtually nothing. There are spelling errors, as well as word choice (*close/clothes*). There are no supporting examples of any kind.

Score 1 Essay

In my opinion, should we install more surveillance cameras in public places? I think, "yes," is a good idea. Why or why not? In my opinion, it is for making ensured the safety in places such as parking lots. This is what our write to privacy can do and tell the law enforcement officials and government too.

Scoring evaluation: Besides being too short, repetitive, and not answering the actual essay question, this essay is almost incomprehensible.

9. Today's top professional athletes often have salaries and bonuses in the tens of millions of dollars. Golfer Tiger Woods makes more than $80 million per year and football pro Peyton Manning makes over $42 million.

   Assignment: Do you think these athletes deserve such high compensation? Plan your response and support your position with specific points and examples from your observations, studies, reading, or personal experiences.

Score 6 Essay

When he was at the height of his basketball career, Michael Jordan was making approximately $300,000 per game. That's more than most people make in a year; indeed, it's more than some people earn in a lifetime. Yes, Michael Jordan was a phenomenal basketball player. Yes, he was also a fantastic role model. But no, he did not deserve to earn such a ridiculously high salary. Jordan, like many other top professional athletes, was grossly overpaid.

Why do top athletes earn such inflated salaries? Because they bring big bucks into their cities and franchises. But what sort of service do they provide to society? Do they save lives? No. Do they improve the standard of living or promote positive social change? No. Do they help keep our streets safe or educate our kids? No. True, many of the top athletes are good role models for our children. But seven-figure salaries don't always mean model behavior. Take N.B.A. star Latrell Sprewell, for example, who choked and threatened to kill his coach.

It is true that professional athletes work hard, and many have spent their lives pursuing their goals. It is also true that most professional athletes have a relatively short career span—a decade perhaps at the top of their game. Limited as their professional sporting career may be, they don't deserve such high salaries. After their professional sports careers are over, they can certainly pursue other careers and work "regular" jobs like the rest of us. Ending their stint as professional athletes doesn't mean they have to stop earning incomes. They just have to earn incomes in a different way. Why should they be any different from the rest of us who may need to switch careers?

It is also true that professional athletes may be injured while on the job; their work is indeed physical, and especially in contact sports like football, injuries are bound to happen. But, like the rest of us, they have insurance, and in nearly all cases, their exorbitant salaries more than cover their medical costs. And theirs is not the only high-risk job. What about miners, construction workers, or firefighters? They are at risk for physical injury every day, too—injuries that could likewise end their careers. But they sure aren't earning millions of dollars a year.

It is also true that professional athletes may spend years and years practicing with farm teams for a fraction of the salary they receive once they make it to the top. But in every career path, we start off with lower wages and must pay our dues and work our way up. Besides, farm team salaries are not always so low.

We're a sports-crazy country, a nation of fanatic sports fans and celebrity worshippers. We're awed and entertained by the best of them—the Michael Jordans, the Alex Rodriguezes, the Emmitt Smiths. But as much as they may inspire and amuse us, professional athletes do not deserve such high salaries. Those millions could be much more wisely spent.

Scoring evaluation: This student uses such strong examples that his or her essay is quite persuasive. There is a clear introduction, body, and conclusion and a great use of sentence variety and vocabulary. Since it is free of any grammatical, usage, or spelling errors as well, it is clear why this essay would score a 6.

Score 5 Essay

The question of whether or not professional athletes are paid too much is really not debatable; virtually everyone who is asked is sure to agree on the subject. Of course they are paid too much, often obscenely so. But as much as people may protest and complain, many of them are the very same people who happily shell out money not only for tickets to see these athletes perform, but also money to cable companies to watch live games and big bucks for the multiple products they endorse. In many ways, this seems hypocritical to me.

In our society, economy is usually a case of supply and demand. It is the same with sports, in my opinion. These athletes could never command the immense salaries they do if thousands of fans were not willing to support them in multiple ways. The fans demand the tickets, the games, and the products and so the sports stars supply it, earning huge incomes in the process. If these same fans turn around and whine about the athletes' enormous pay checks, their complaints seem hollow and insincere, in my opinion.

Perhaps the key to limiting athlete's salaries lies with the fans themselves. While I am not a sports enthusiast myself, I can see that it could possibly be influential if fans would simply say no to paying high prices for tickets, games, and products. If they stopped buying them and perhaps even followed up this voluntary boycott with letters to the editor of sports magazines and other publications, changes might occur down the line. Perhaps this is simply wishful thinking or false optimism, but I like to think that the little people can make a real difference.

Professional athletes are commonly paid millions of dollars every year, making far more money than the average person will ever see in an entire lifetime, including myself. Do they earn it? There is little question that they worked hard to reach their level of skill and are extraordinarily talented at what they do, but in a world where people like teachers, social workers, and other community workers can hardly make ends meet, the fairness of their salaries is decidedly debatable.

Scoring evaluation: This essay is an example of a student who wrote on a somewhat unfamiliar topic (he or she is not a sports fan) but in a convincing and logical manner. It has great vocabulary; good examples; and a clear introduction, body, and conclusion. Although the writer would benefit from not qualifying some of

his or her statements ("in my opinion"), this essay is a strong one that would easily get a good score.

Score 4 Essay

Do athletes get paid too much? You bet. That's my opinion. Professional athletes, what do they do with all that money? Imagine Michael Jordan earning $300,000 per game! Plus all his money from Nike and other advertising. I think that money can be put to much better use in this country.

Professional athletes should get good salaries, but not the millions like they get now. It's just too much. Their job isn't dangerous, except maybe for football or ice hockey where it's easy to get a bad injury. It's easy to get a bad injury in lots of other jobs, too, like construction, but they don't get millions of dollars. I guess, the difference is that nobody likes to watch construction workers. There's fun in the game and people like the competition, sports teams bring lots of money into a city's economy.

If professional athletes could guarantee they'd also be a good role model for kids, then maybe they could have such high salaries. Because they'd be doing something good for society since so many kids are watching. For now though, it's too much.

Scoring evaluation: There is a lot of rambling in this essay. When you add in spelling errors, repetition, little sentence variety, and grammar mistakes, you can see why this would only earn a 4.

Score 3 Essay

Can you imagine getting paid hundreds of thousands of dollars for just a few hours of your time? Wouldn't that be nice? I guess so. Professional athletes do. How can they be worth all of that? I don't get it.

Of course, people like Tiger Woods and Michael Jordan are very talented. They worked hard to reach the level they are. I don't doubt that for one minute.

But do they deserve to be paid millions of dollars every year? I personally say no way.

I like to watch sports. I appreciate the talent that goes into being able to play like that. Of course, if I could make the much money doing it, I would be willing to practice a little more often myself. Then I could make too much money and people could complain alot about me.

Scoring evaluation: This essay sounds like a phone conversation between two friends, rather than an essay that is supposed to have an introduction, body, and conclusion with supporting examples. It strays from the main topic and is too informal for the assignment.

Score 2 Essay

Wow, these people sure do make a lot of money. It must be nice to never have to worry about paying for things. Like we do. Maybe I should practece more often to.

Are they paid too much? Yeah. I sure do think so. They make as much from making tv commercials than playing games. That stinks. Other people deserve to make that much. Like teachers. Like ministers. Or maybe the people who make sure kids find parents to adopt them.

In conclusion, I believe that athleets do not deserve this high compensation at all. It is not fair.

Scoring evaluation: This essay attempts to answer the question but gets completely bogged down in fragments, misspelled words, and irrelevant examples.

Score 1 Essay

Today the athleets so much money. Millions an millions of the dollars. They playing baseball, basketball; football, even for golf. This is the not of the dangerous sport, even less than many of the others.

The money, it's too much, giving mine opinon. For the teems and the citys its so much there's else to

pay for with the money, like homelessness. This is the need to be changed.

Scoring evaluation: Like other essays that only score a 1 on the SAT, this one is almost incomprehensible due to errors. It is not clear what the student is attempting to say, and the essay is too full of flaws to make any sense.

11. According to the National Center for Statistics and Analysis of the National Highway Traffic Safety Administration, at any given moment during the day, 974,000 cars on the road are being driven by a person talking on a cell phone. Some states have made it illegal to do this. Other states are giving the idea some thought.

> **Assignment:** Should it be illegal for the driver of a vehicle to use a cell phone? Plan your response and support your position with specific points and examples from your observations, studies, reading, or personal experiences.

Score 6 Essay

No matter how careful a driver you may be, when you do something else while driving, whether it's drinking coffee, changing the radio station, looking at a map, or making a call on your cell phone, you endanger yourself and others because you are distracted from your driving. Even a fraction of a second of distraction is enough to cause an accident. While no state can make it illegal to drink coffee or switch stations while driving, all states can, and should, make it illegal to drive while talking on a cellular phone.

In the past decade, as the popularity of cellular phones has risen, so have the number of accidents caused by people talking on their cell phones. Whether they were dialing a number, listening to a message, or simply in a heated conversation, they were momentarily distracted from the task of driving, and suddenly—crash! Fortunately, many of these accidents have been minor fender-benders.

But all too many have been deadly accidents that could have been prevented by a stricter cell-phone use laws.

Cell phone proponents may argue that talking on a cell phone is no more dangerous than, for example, having a cup of coffee while on the road or talking to someone in the back seat. But unlike a cup of coffee, which you can put down between sips, you must keep the phone in your hand. That means that you have only one hand on the wheel while you're driving. That makes cell phones doubly dangerous: Not only are you distracted by dialing or by the conversation, but you are also driving one-handed, which means you are less in control. If you suddenly need both hands on the wheel to prevent an accident or to keep your car from sliding, the extra second it takes to get your hand back on the wheel can make the difference between an accident and an accident narrowly averted or between a serious injury and a minor one.

Cell phones are also dangerous because when you are busy talking, especially if you really have to concentrate on the matter you are discussing, your mind is not fully focused on the road, and this has a significant effect on your reaction time. You will be slower to make important driving decisions such as how soon to brake and when to switch lanes, and you will be less able to respond to situations on the road.

Many people use cell phones to report accidents and emergencies, to let loved ones know they'll be late, and to stay in touch when they're out of town. I'm not arguing that you shouldn't have a cell phone in your car. What I am saying is that you shouldn't be driving when you're talking on that phone. Until your state outlaws hand-held cell phones in cars, pull over to the side of the road when you are ready to make a call. It may add a few extra minutes to your commute, but it just might save your life.

Scoring evaluation: Anyone who reads this can spot that this is a very strong essay. It uses a wide variety of sentence structure and an impressive vocabulary. Spelling and grammar mistakes are absent. The student makes a very strong case against using a cell phone while driving and implementing laws for that reason. Supporting details are significant, and each point is very relevant to the question asked.

Score 5 Essay

Although driving while talking on a cell phone can be potentially quite dangerous, I think that making it illegal is taking the issue way too far. Instead, I think that cell phone companies need to focus on alternative products that will still allow people to access the convenience of a cell phone without the risk.

Several years ago, in response to a rising concern about the danger of talking on a cell phone while behind the wheel, a number of companies began producing cell phones that could be mounted to the dash. This kept drivers' hands free, but still allowed them to make calls and talk to friends, family, and business associates as needed. Unfortunately, this did not always produce the sound quality some wanted and so other options are still needed.

I believe that cell phone companies are going to create innovative new options before a law against using a cell while driving is passed throughout the country. Several possibilities are already emerging on the market. For example, some people have a product that they attach to their ears and connect remotely to the cell phone. Using this, they can talk and listen while keeping both hands on the wheel and maintain high quality sound.

In the near future, I imagine that other high-tech phones will be invented to be used hands-free. I can even picture a day where cell phone technology is implanted under our skin or are installed as part of typical new car design. I hope that these kinds of things happen before the law banning them is passed. I feel that it is too extreme a reaction and that cell phones are too much a part of our daily routines to go without.

Scoring evaluation: This is also a strong essay with some good points supporting the idea of being able to use a cell phone safely. The examples are strong, and the vocabulary is excellent. There is sentence variety throughout, and everything focuses on answering the main question.

Score 4 Essay

Driving with a cell phone is dangerous, and it should be illegal. Its all ready illegal in some states, in my opinion it, should be illegal in all of them.

First of all, driving with a cell phone is dangerous because your distracted. Especially when you're dialing a number, then you're not even looking at the road. What if the cars in front of you suddenly stop?

You can also be distracted by the conversation you are having and lose focus from driving. This means that you may not be able to react quick enough to dangers on the road. Another problem is that with a cell phone, you don't have both hands on the wheel, and that's for the whole time you're talking. You can't make sharp turns and handle sudden curves with just one hand.

Lots of people think, oh, it's just one quick call, no problem. But even just a quick call makes you distracted, even just for a quick second. That's enough to cause an accident. So don't drive when you need to talk on your cell phone. Instead, be safe and pull over.

Scoring evaluation: Although this student has some good points to make, some of the meaning is lost because of the multitude of errors, ranging from spelling to misuse of an adverb (*quick/quickly*) to word choice (*all ready/already*). All of this pulls the score down, as does the overall lack of vocabulary and length.

Score 3 Essay

Talking on the cell phone while you are behind the wheel is not only stupid and annoying but dangerous as well. I don't know why people do it. It really makes me mad. I see it on the rode all the time.

I do not live in one of the states who has made it illegal. I wish I did. I would vote for it. I would, for sure. I don't get why people feel they have to talk while they are diving. Can't they wait? I mean, you will be out of the car soon so why not just wait until then? How hard can it be?

Perhaps people could get the kind of cell phone that mounts on the dash. That is an improvement. At least your hands are free. You could also let a passenger do the talking for you. This way you would keep your eyes on traffic where they should be at all times.

So, in conclusion, yes, it should be made illegal. That is just common sense. I hope it is a law that gets passed very soon.

Scoring evaluation: Like others you've read, this student uses a lot of space to say very little. The sentences are choppy, examples are missing completely, and there is an enormous amount of repetition.

Score 2 Essay

It is dangerous enuf to drive on most rodes today without adding the problem of cell phones. Why do people do it? It is not smart. It is dumb. It should be illegal. So, yes, I believe it should be ilegal to talk on a cell phone while driving.

I have watched my dad talk on the phone while he drives. He does not pay attention like he should. He misses things. I had to warn him once to stop. That proves it to me. It realy does. So make it ilegal. That is my opinion on cell phones and driving.

Scoring evaluation: It is challenging to fill up those lines when you have not thought out what you want to say as this student has done. Although there is an opinion with one supporting example, there is no sense of introduction, body, or conclusion. It reads more like rambling than answering a question.

Score 1 Essay

In many states of the United States they make it again the law for talking while driving with cellular telephone. In my opinion, is this a good idea? I believe.

For to many accidents, are happening with the cellular telephone, the driver he don't see (what happens) ahead. This terrible for every one especial the ones they getting hurt. Some accident really very terrible and, everyone going to the hospital. This should be the law.

Scoring evaluation: Like the others with this score, this essay is so full of errors that it is hard to understand what is being said. Verb tenses, word choices, grammar, spelling, and form are all lost.

18. One of the biggest educational trends in recent years is homeschooling. It is growing each year by approximately 15%. More than one million children of all ages are currently being educated at home.

> **Assignment:** Do you think that homeschooling is a valuable educational method? Plan your response and support your position with specific points and examples from your observations, studies, reading, or personal experiences.

Score 6 Essay

I firmly believe that the only way we can make wise decisions in life to make informed decisions. Many of the people who form opinions about homeschooling know little to nothing about it. Instead, they base their perceptions on common myths, inaccurate assumptions, and idle gossip. I am personally a strong advocate of homeschooling because I have experienced it on a daily basis; I was homeschooled for five years.

When my parents first broached the topic with me, I responded quite negatively. I raised the most common objections: It could not be legal; I would never have anyone to play with; I would be horrendously bored staying home all the time and certainly my parents could never provide the same high quality education I would get in public school. Despite my vocal and vehement arguments, my parents were determined homeschooling was the best option for my education. To reach a compromise, we agreed to try it for only a few months and then reevaluate. I was sure that when that time came, we would mutually agree that it had been a disastrous decision.

Now I can look back at the whole experience and realize how naïve and uneducated I once was about homeschooling. I had fallen prey to the same misconceptions that people continue to believe today. During my five years of homeschooling, I researched the topic, through books, websites, and even regional and national conferences. What I learned—far outside of my daily curriculum—was that homeschooling is one of the best educational options families have today. Instead of being illegal, it was legal in all states. Instead of being lonely and bored at home, I was immersed in classes, workshops, pot lucks, meetings, and play dates many times each week. I made multiple new friends and continued to see my public school friends on the weekends. My education was high quality; indeed, I feel I learned more in those five years than I could possibly have learned in school. Best of all, I was allowed the time to pursue some of my deepest passions, from drama and theater to foreign languages. I discovered a true love of learning and realized that, as Winston Churchill once said, "I am always ready to learn but I do not always like being taught."

Today, I try to remind myself to never make a hasty judgment about any controversial issue without doing some research. Forming an opinion about something I personally know nothing of is foolhardy. Too often, I suspect later I might have to eat those words.

Scoring evaluation: The writer of this essay has a strong opinion about the issue and makes that clear through the powerful examples he or she uses. The introduction, body, and conclusion are all clearly stated, and there is excellent sentence variety and vocabulary use.

Score 5 Essay

While a large number of families are choosing to homeschool today, I think it is a mistake. I believe they do it for logical and understandable reasons, but in my opinion, the negative aspects outweigh any of the positive ones. Homeschooling keeps kids from making friends, playing sports, and getting into college.

If kids spend all of their time at home, how can they begin to learn the socialization skills that they will eventually need for coping with people on the job or other situations? All young people need time to be with friends, whether studying, talking, or just being together. Families are wonderful but friends are equally essential. If kids do not attend school, they will not get the opportunity to socialize.

Many kids want to play some kind of sports and once again, by not enrolling in a public school, they will not have the chance. How many future sports stars are lost because these young people never get the chance to kick a ball, swing a bat, or race around the track? Regular physical exercise is a vital part of good health and once again, these kids are missing out.

Lastly, homeschooled students will never be able to get into college. They will not have the school records, grade point averages, or test scores that college applications require. Moreover, they would

never be able to handle the college lifestyle after being so isolated in their homes all of their lives.

Ralph Waldo Emerson once wrote that "The secret of education lies in respecting the pupil." I think that homeschooling shows no respect at all but in fact, shows disrespect for the wants and needs of all students.

Scoring evaluation: This is a strong essay based on a strong opinion. The examples cited are relevant and flow with good organization from one to the next. The question is answered solidly, and there is good sentence variety and vocabulary use. The quote at the end is an excellent touch and ties the rest of the essay together.

Score 4 Essay

If you had asked me this question last year, I would most likely have told you that homeschooling was not a good option for kids. I would have based this opinion on little more than rumors and stories I have seen on television about it. Today, I can give you a better opinion because my best friend is homeschooled and I have learned a lot about it as we got to know each other.

When I first met Nicole, I had no idea she was homeschooled. She was taking a soccer class at the YMCA and so was I. She seemed really nice and before long, we were talking on the phone after class and getting together to do things on the weekends. When I finally realized she was homeschooled, I couldn't believe it. She seemed so normal. Since then, I have learned that homeschoolers are just like you and me, they just learn in different ways.

In some ways, I envy Nicole. She gets to sleep in in the mornings and never has to deal with riding the bus, which I hate doing. She gets a lot of time to read whatever she wants. That would be nice. On the other hand, she spends a lot of time with her mother and her two brothers and I am not sure how I would feel about that because I think I would get tired of that.

Nicole has shown me that there are a lot of different ways to learn information. When I told her about a Shakespearian play we read in English class, she told me she had read it too and loved it. Later, she got me tickets to go and see it.

Homeschooling certainly is not for everyone. I am not sure if I would like it or not but I do believe it works well for some familys, like Nicoles. She is a very smart and fun person and she has taught me an important lesson: not to judge people until I really know what they are like.

Scoring evaluation: This is a pretty good essay with a strong opinion, supported by a personal example that is relevant. The vocabulary use is not as good as it could be, and there are some punctuation, spelling, and usage errors that interfere with the essay's readability.

Score 3 Essay

I cannot believe that more than one million kids are being homeschooled today I had no idea the number was so high. I have heard a lot about homeschooling. It is on the news and in the newspaper a lot. Some of the stories say how good these students do, others just say these people are not being watched carefully enough and are committing crimes.

A good education is important. You probably can get it in several ways. That inclues homeschooling. I think that parents have to be very dedicated to their kids. Families spend a lot of time together. I wouldn't mind that part. I don't see very much of my family during the week. We are all going in opposite directions. I miss them.

I think that homeschooling can be a good idea if parents do it right. Research it carefully. Make sure their kids are keeping up in all subjects. Make sure their kids get time to play with friends and do fun stuff, rather than just stay home and study all of the time. So, I guess, in conclusion, if done properly, then going to school at home can be a smart idea, in my opinion.

Scoring evaluation: There are some good thoughts here, but they simply are not developed enough. More details and examples are needed to make it longer and give it support. The writer strays from the topic several times into areas that are not pertinent, and there is not much sense of an introduction and body in this example.

Score 2 Essay

Homeschooling, is it a good idea? I don't know. I think it depends. Some families might do it well. Not others. They do not know what they are doing. They didn't go to college to be teachers they are parents.

I wouldn't mind trying it. Might be inneresting. If I got to sleep in each day that would be the best part.

There are some homeschoolers in my soccer class at the Y. They seem nice enough. They don't look any different from anyone else.

So, yes, I think homeschooling is a good idea. If it is done right, that is.

Scoring evaluation: This student is just rambling and has no sense of organization or support for what he or she is saying. Spelling and usage errors are prevalent and make the essay hard to read and understand.

Score 1 Essay

Homeschooled kids learn nuthin. I think there lazy. They probly get to do anything they want. I wanna do that (not go to school). Sounds fun.

I bet you can't go to college. If your homeschooled. Why would you wanna go anyway? I think home schooling is a big mistake you should not do it.

Scoring evaluation: Once again, this level of essay leaves the reader confused and trying to unscramble the meaning behind the mistakes. There is no support for the student's opinion; there is no introduction, body, or conclusion; and no sentence variety or vocabulary use. There is almost nothing here to use for scoring purposes.

Posttest ▶

Now is your chance to shine and prove all that you have learned throughout this book. It's time for the posttest. Sharpen your pencil, take a deep breath, and go. Good luck!

Like the pretest, the posttest will include:

- 9 identifying sentence error questions
- 12 improving sentences questions
- 3 improving paragraphs questions
- 1 writing prompt

POSTTEST

1. a b c d e
2. a b c d e
3. a b c d e
4. a b c d e
5. a b c d e
6. a b c d e
7. a b c d e
8. a b c d e
9. a b c d e
10. a b c d e

11. a b c d e
12. a b c d e
13. a b c d e
14. a b c d e
15. a b c d e
16. a b c d e
17. a b c d e
18. a b c d e
19. a b c d e
20. a b c d e

21. a b c d e
22. a b c d e
23. a b c d e
24. a b c d e

▶ Questions

The following sentences test your knowledge of grammar, usage, diction, and idiom. Some sentences are correct as is. No sentence has more than one error. You will find the error, if there is one, underlined and lettered. Elements of the sentence that are not underlined will not be changed. In choosing answers, follow the requirements of standard written English. If there is an error, select the one underlined part that must be changed to make the sentence correct. If there is no error, select choice **e**.

1. After watching both versions of *King Kong,* my family declared that the original was the dullest. No error.
      a   b   c   d   e

2. Chocolate chip oatmeal cookies, which are sold in the bakery just around the corner,
                                        a   b
is my favorite afternoon treat during the winter. No error.
         c   d   e

3. I could not believe it when my mother told me that school had been cancelled for the rest of the week
        a   b   c
because the measles was going around. No error.
             d   e

4. The photographs and the captions for the high school's yearbook goes into the editor's mail slot in the
             a   b   c
main administrative office. No error.
         d   e

5. Because the history professor was exceptionally late, the vast majority of the students leave the room.
             a   b   c   d
No error.
  e

6. Occasionally, some divorcing couples will choose a disinterested third party to help them figure out the
                            a   b   c
financial and custodial aspects of their new arrangement. No error.
                          d   e

7. Elisa can write good, so it came as no surprise whatsoever when she won the regional essay contest
             a   b   c
sponsored by the community college. No error.
    d   e

8. Recent <u>studies have shown</u> that <u>children who drink</u> an <u>inordinate amount</u> of soda

           a   **b**   **c**

<u>frequent avoid drinking water</u> or fruit juices. <u>No error.</u>

         d   **e**

9. Karen or Sarah <u>will raise</u> <u>their hands</u> to let you know when <u>it is the perfect time</u> to make <u>your appearance</u>.

                          a   **b**   **c**   **d**

<u>No error.</u>

    e

The following sentences test correctness and effectiveness of expression. In choosing answers, follow the requirements of standard written English; in other words, pay attention to grammar, choice of words, sentence construction, and punctuation.

In each of the following sentences, part of the sentence or the entire sentence is underlined. Beneath each sentence, you will find five options for phrasing that underlined part. Choice **a** repeats the original, so if you believe it is correct as is, this is the correct answer. Your choice should produce the most effective sentence—clear and precise, without awkwardness or ambiguity.

10. The overall decrease in traditional public school funding is occasionally attributed to the steady <u>growth of homeschooling, it is increasing</u> at an average of 15% per year.
   a. growth of homeschooling, it is increasing
   b. growth of homeschooling it is increasing
   c. growth of homeschooling; it is increasing
   d. growth of homeschooling, but it is increasing
   e. growth of homeschooling, although it
      is increasing

11. Although he stated earlier that he had planned to retire from writing nonstop best-sellers, <u>Stephen King's newest release titled *The Cell.*</u>
   a. Stephen King's newest release titled *The Cell.*
   b. Stephen King's newest release is titled *The Cell.*
   c. Stephen King's newest release, which is titled *The Cell.*
   d. Stephen King's newest release known as *The Cell.*
   e. Stephen King's newest release are titled *The Cell.*

12. <u>A classic novel was removed from the required reading list that was considered to be far too controversial and racist for the majority of the students.</u>

   a. A classic novel was removed from the required reading list that was considered to be far too controversial and racist for the majority of the students.

   b. Far too controversial and racist for the major- ity of the students, the list removed the classic novel from required reading.

   c. Considered to be far too controversial and racist by the majority of the students, the required reading list removed the classic novel.

   d. A classic novel that was considered to be far too controversial and racist for the majority of the students was removed from the required reading list.

   e. The majority of students, feeling the classic novel was far too controversial and racist for the required reading list, removed it.

13. The immense mountain ranges of the Pacific Northwest are commonly sprinkled with snow, covered in clouds, <u>and endless evergreen pine trees cover them.</u>

   a. and endless evergreen pine trees cover them.

   b. with pine trees endlessly evergreen covering them.

   c. plus covers in endless evergreen pine trees.

   d. but still endless evergreen pine trees cover them.

   e. and covered with endless evergreen pine trees.

14. Although the cost of fossil fuels has continued to rise and people have vehemently protested, <u>but consumers just keep paying the exorbitant prices and filling up their tanks.</u>

   a. but consumers just keep paying the exorbitant prices and filling up their tanks.

   b. paying the exorbitant prices and filling up their tanks, consumers keep doing.

   c. consumers just keep paying the exorbitant prices and filling up their tanks.

   d. and consumers just keep paying the exorbitant prices and filling up their tanks.

   e. exorbitant prices and filling up their tanks, consumers just keep paying and doing

15. While an amazing number of bands from the 1960s and 1970s have tried to reunite for touring purposes, <u>they rarely are as successful as they had hoped.</u>

   a. they rarely are as successful as they had hoped.

   b. so they rarely are as successful as they had hoped.

   c. rarely as successful as they had hoped are they.

   d. because they had hoped to be as successful.

   e. that they rarely are as successful as they hoped to be.

16. Since e-mails have become such a popular and convenient method of personal and business communication, <u>so old-fashioned letter writing is becoming a lost art.</u>
  a. so old-fashioned letter writing is becoming a lost art.
  b. old-fashioned letter writing is becoming a lost art.
  c. because old-fashioned letter writing has become a lost art.
  d. old-fashioned letter writing will become a lost art.
  e. however, old-fashioned letter writing is becoming a lost art.

17. A variety of Broadway shows have been attracting huge audiences and reviving the concept of <u>live theatre, *Wicked* and *Mama Mia*</u> brought in a record number of new fans.
  a. live theatre, *Wicked* and *Mama Mia*
  b. live theatre *Wicked* and *Mama Mia*
  c. live theatre, but *Wicked* and *Mama Mia*
  d. live theatre, however, *Wicked* and *Mama Mia*
  e. live theatre; *Wicked* and *Mama Mia*

18. Led by such well-known rockers as Rod Stewart, crooning <u>ballads from the 1940s and 1950s, a large and unexpected comeback</u> with baby boomers.
  a. ballads from the 1940s and 1950s, a large and unexpected comeback
  b. ballads from the 1940s and 1950s; a large and unexpected comeback
  c. ballads from the 1940s and 1950s are making a large and unexpected comeback
  d. ballads from the 1940s and 1950s makes a large and unexpected comeback
  e. ballads from the 1940s and 1950s will be making a large and unexpected comeback

19. The new museum offers everything from submarine tours, planetarium shows, science lab demonstrations, <u>and interactive exhibits, children converge</u> on the place daily.
  a. and interactive exhibits, children converge
  b. and interactive exhibits, but children converge
  c. and interactive exhibits children converge
  d. and interactive exhibits; children converge
  e. and interactive exhibits which children converge

20. <u>Today's growing industry of alternative medicine offers consumers healthier choices, more natural treatments, wider options, and healthcare professionals who truly care.</u>
  a. Today's growing industry of alternative medicine offers consumers healthier choices, more natural treatments, wider options, and healthcare professionals who truly care.
  b. Today's growing industry of alternative medicine offers consumers healthier choices, more natural treatments, wider options, and truly caring healthcare professionals.
  c. Today's growing industry of alternative medicine offers consumers healthier choices, naturaller treatments, wider options, and truly caring healthcare professionals.
  d. Today's growing industry of alternative medicine offers consumers more healthy choices, more natural treatments, more wide options and more caring professionals in healthcare.
  e. Today's growing industry of alternative medicine offers consumers healthier choices, more natural treatments, wider options, and healthcare professionals that are truly caring.

21. Because he had already finished his research paper three weeks before it was due, <u>Jason spent his entire weekend reading and relaxing.</u>

a. Jason spent his entire weekend reading and relaxing.

b. so Jason spent his entire weekend reading and relaxing.

c. but Jason spent his entire weekend reading and relaxing.

d. although Jason spent his entire weekend reading and relaxing

e. since Jason spent his entire weekend reading and relaxing.

The following passage is an early draft of a student's essay, and parts of it need to be rewritten. Read the passage and answer the questions that follow it. Some questions are about individual sentences or parts of sentences. Here, you are asked to select the choice that will improve the sentence structure and word choice. Other questions refer to parts of the essay or even the entire essay and ask you to look carefully at its organization and development. You should follow the conventions of standard written English in answering the questions.

(1) Charles Dickens wrote an amazing number of books in his lifetime. (2) Before they were put into book format, however, they were published in magazines, one chapter at a time. (3) This kept readers subscribing to the publications. (4) Whenever one of his stories appeared, the number of copies sold would skyrocket.

(5) Dickens was much like the Stephen King of the 1800s. (6) Every single one of his books was a best-seller. (7) People followed the author on the street. (8) They wanted to meet him. (9) They were curious about him. (10) Many of his characters were as well known as television actors are today. (11) If a beloved character died in one of his stories, fans mourned to the point of even refusing to go to work or school.

(12) Although Dickens was an amazingly successful author, it was the stage that was his true passion. (13) He loved acting in live theatre, and during the last decade of his life, he performed excerpts from his own books to captivated audiences around the world.

22. Which of the following is the best way to combine sentences 7, 8, and 9 (reproduced below)?

People followed the author on the street. They wanted to meet him. They were curious about him.

a. People followed the author on the street, wanting to meet him as they were curious about him.

b. People followed the author on the street because they were curious and wanted to meet him.

c. Following the author on the street, people wanted to meet him because they were curious.

d. Because they wanted to meet him, people followed the author on the street because they were curious about him.

e. They wanted to meet him and were curious, so people followed the author on the street.

23. Which sentence most appropriately follows sentence 13?

   a. Even when his health was declining, Dickens continued to perform some of the most violent and emotional acts from his books.

   b. He is most well known for his holiday classic, *A Christmas Carol,* which has been turned into many different plays and films.

   c. In fact, when a children's character named Little Nell died in one novel, people were seen crying in the middle of the street with the magazine in their hands.

   d. In fact, Dickens was considered the wealthiest and most popular author of his generation.

   e. It was where he felt like he was truly in his element and could show all of the emotion he put into his stories.

24. This passage discusses everything EXCEPT

   a. how fans responded to Dickens's stories.

   b. the overwhelming popularity of Dickens's books.

   c. Dickens's fascination with performing.

   d. where Dickens's stories were published.

   e. the background of Dickens's family and poverty.

25. Activist Jeannette Rankin once said, "You can no more win a war than you can win an earthquake."

   Assignment: Do you agree or disagree with this statement? Plan your response and support your position with specific points and examples from your observations, studies, reading, or personal experiences.

▶ Answers

1. d. This sentence has an error in comparison. When two things are compared, the comparative degree (ending in *-er* or using the word *more*) is used, rather than the superlative degree (ending in *-est* or using the word *most*).

2. c. This sentence has an error with subject-verb agreement. The subject is *cookies*, which is plural, so the verb *is* should be changed to the plural *are*.

3. d. There are some subject words that are singular, but they appear to be plural because they end in *-s*. An example of this is *measles*. The verb should be *was* instead of *were*.

4. c. When two nouns are joined by an *and*, they are considered compound subjects and require plural verbs. *Goes* should be *go*.

5. d. The problem here is verb tense. The first verb is *was*, indicating the past tense. The second verb should also be in the past tense to be consistent. *Leave* should be *left*.

6. e. There is no error in this sentence.

7. a. The word *good* is an adjective, and it should not be used after most verbs (unless they are linking verbs). *Good* should be replaced with *well*.

8. d. This is an error with using an adverb. The word *frequent* is modifying the verb *avoid*. It should be *frequently*.

9. b. When singular antecedents (*Karen* and *Sarah*) are joined by *or* or *nor* as in this sentence, the pronoun that follows should also be singular. *Their* should be *her*.

10. c. This is an example of a run-on sentence, or two complete sentences improperly joined. To be repaired, you either need to insert a semicolon or the appropriate coordinating conjunction. The two coordinating conjunctions offered here (*although* and *but*) do not connect the two clauses logically.

11. b. This is a sentence fragment, because the independent clause contains no verb. Both choices **b** and **e** supply a verb, but choice **e** is incorrect because the noun is singular and *are* is a plural verb.

12. d. This is a case of a misplaced modifier. The list is not what was controversial and racist; the classic novel is. The modifying clause should be next to *novel*, not *list*, as in choice **d**.

13. e. This is a case of faulty parallelism. There are three verb clauses here. With the first two clauses, the pattern is verb-preposition-noun, but the last phrase does not follow this pattern.

14. c. In this example, you have a cause of faulty coordination. The two parts of the sentence do not fit together. The first part is a dependent clause and it must be followed by an independent clause. Because the second part of the sentence begins with *but*, however, it is also dependent. The conjunction needs to be removed, as in choice **c**.

15. a. There is no error in this sentence.

16. b. In this sentence, there is faulty coordination. You have a dependent clause followed by another dependent clause. By removing the *so*, you have corrected the problem. Some choices replace the *so* with another conjunction, which repeats the problem. The other choice changes the verb tense and makes the sentence awkward.

17. e. This is a run-on sentence, so the two parts need to be separated by either an appropriate conjunction or a semicolon. The insertion of *but* or *however* does not make sense with the rest of the sentence, so the only correct answer is choice **e**, which adds the semicolon.

18. c. This sentence is a fragment missing a verb. Punctuation does not correct it; it needs to have a verb in the proper tense added.

19. d. This is a run-on sentence that needs to be broken into two parts or joined together with the appropriate conjunction. Only choice **d** does this. The addition of *but* or *which* does not fix the problem, as one obscures the meaning and the other creates a dependent clause.

20. b. This is an example of faulty parallelism. The pattern established in the sentence is for an adjective followed by a noun, and the last example breaks this pattern.

21. a. There is no error in this question.

22. b. This is a combination question. Choice **b** is the only one that combines all three sentences in a way that is not awkward or wordy.

23. a. This is a content question. Although all the choices would fit into the essay at some point, only choice **a** is directly related to the same topic as sentence 13.

24. e. All the topics mentioned in the choices were mentioned in the essay, except for the topic in choice **e**.

25. Answers will vary.

Special Offer from LearningExpress!

Let LearningExpress help you acquire essential writing skills FAST

 Go to the LearningExpress Practice Center at www.LearningExpressFreeOffer.com, an interactive online resource exclusively for LearningExpress customers.

Now that you've purchased LearningExpress's 411 SAT Essay Prompts and Writing Questions, you have **FREE** access to:

- **49 pratice questions** in identifying sentence errors, improving sentences, and improving paragraphs
- **A FREE online essay** to practice your narrative essay writing-instantly scored
- **Immediate scoring** and **detailed answer explanations**
- Benchmark your skills and focus your study with our **customized diagnostic report**

Follow the simple instructions on the scratch card in your copy of *411 SAT Essay Prompts and Writing Questions.* Use your individualized access code found on the scratch card and go to www.LearningExpressFreeOffer.com to sign in. Start practicing your writing skills online right away!

Once you've logged on, use the spaces below to write in your access code and newly created password for easy reference:

Access Code: _____   Password: _____